FROM STRESS

to

STILLNESS

FROM STRESS

to

STILLNESS

Tools for Inner Peace

GINA LAKE

Endless Satsang Foundation

www.RadicalHappiness.com

Cover photograph: © arvitalya/iStockPhoto.com

ISBN: 978-1477646656

Copyright © 2013 by Gina Lake

CONTENTS

INTRODUCTION

Although many of the things that cause stress are out of our control, much of our stress is caused by what we say to ourselves and by what we believe about ourselves, about life, and about others. This is something we *do* have some control over. My intention in writing this is to bring more awareness to the types of thoughts that create stress and offer practices and suggestions that will lead to living in greater peace and equanimity, even in a busy, competitive, and stressful world.

Most people are well aware of how stress undermines their happiness, effectiveness, and relationships. More are also becoming aware of the toll it takes on the body. When we're under stress, whether that stress is coming from the environment or from our own internal self-talk, the body releases stress hormones. which compromise the body's ability to regenerate and fend off disease. Even the brain is affected by stress, as the forebrain shuts down and a more primitive part of our brain takes over, resulting in less intelligent action.

Because the body doesn't distinguish between actual threats and imagined ones (both cause a release of stress hormones), it's important that we don't add stress to our already stressful lives by imagining worst-case scenarios and giving our attention to negative thoughts. Being absorbed in such thoughts only weakens us—literally—and makes us less effective and less happy.

Although we can't do anything about fearful and other negative thoughts arising, since producing such thoughts is just what our brains do, we can disengage from such thoughts once we realize they aren't serving us. This book is intended to help you do that. We have the ability to become aware of what we're thinking and to determine if a thought is helping or hindering us. This capacity empowers us to stop believing and acting on thoughts that don't serve us. Learning to be this aware and to act this consciously isn't necessarily easy, but it gets easier the more we practice it.

As we will see, believing fears and other thoughts that create stress and tightness in our body is neither functional nor healthy, but dysfunctional and unhealthy, and only leads to unhappiness. We are programmed to believe our thoughts without questioning them, particularly our fearful ones, even though believing them doesn't actually help us survive or be happy, but quite the opposite. In this way, we are wired backwards. This is the source of so much suffering. The thoughts that run through our mind are part of our antiquated programming as a human animal, and these thoughts aren't wise. They don't represent our deeper wisdom, which has little to do with these types of thoughts.

We have many behaviors, habits, and ways of thinking that are part of our programming, which undermine our health, well-being, and happiness. Fortunately, we're able to become conscious of these programmed ways of thinking and being, and thereby become free of them. As we evolve as human beings and become more aware of this dysfunctional programming, many are choosing to disengage from such thoughts.

Awareness is a big step in becoming free of the stress created by believing our fears and other negative thoughts. But awareness alone isn't enough. We will explore ways of moving beyond these thoughts so that living in a state of equanimity becomes easier and more automatic. We will also explore ways you might simplify or restructure your life to minimize any external stressors you might be dealing with.

Reducing stress is so important. It results in being healthier, happier, wiser, more effective, more peaceful, and more loving — because stress robs us of these things. Stress causes us to lose touch with our best self and makes it more likely we'll express our worst self and indulge in destructive habits and addictions. As a result, stress also robs society and those with whom we are in relationship, because how we are in the world matters. It has an impact on everyone and everything around us.

Most of us live very busy lives, and this level of busy-ness is often very stressful. By being so busy, we may be doing a lot and we may even be accomplishing a lot, but at what cost? And of what value is what we're busy with, from the standpoint of our core values? What really matters to you, and how much of your energy is going into those things and how much is being squandered on things that don't really matter, don't make your heart sing, or actually interfere with your emotional, physical, and spiritual well-being?

In our society, doing has become a disease — an addiction — that is robbing us of our soul and, consequently, of our happiness and peace. We'll explore what it's like to honor *being* as much as doing. We'll also explore ways of getting in touch with our beingness: our wise and loving self. When doing flows from being, then the doing is wise, balanced, fulfilling, and serves Life.

Stress keeps us out of touch with our best self and in the grips of the ego, which is the primitive aspect of ourselves that sees the world as dog-eat-dog and something to conquer. This perspective has put our world in peril. What we need now is to be connected to what unifies us as human beings, not what separates us. If we continue to let the ego drive us as individuals, as a society, and as a world, we might not have a world left. So reducing stress is not just about our personal health and well-being, but also about moving society away from conflict and hatred toward what unifies us as human *beings*—toward love. What the world needs now is more love and peace.

For love and peace to blossom in the world, they must first flower within each of us. For this to happen, we need to be willing to examine how we're creating stress and dis-ease within ourselves by believing our thoughts, and we need to be willing to learn to live from a more peaceful and loving place. We need to learn to live from our true being, from what I've often called Essence. For our purposes here, I'll call this place Stillness. It's the place of contentment and the sense that all is well, which we experience whenever our mind is quiet. Stillness is the place of calm, peace, joy, and love at the core of our being. Fortunately, everyone knows what Stillness is, and we're all capable of experiencing it more frequently than we do.

We, as humans, have the capacity for love, peace, and joy or the opposite: hatred, conflict, and unhappiness. All humans experience an inner duality: Our true nature is courageous, kind, compassionate, patient, accepting, and wise; while our false self, the ego, is petty, unkind, fearful, hateful, judgmental, and distrustful of life. Our true nature, fortunately, is goodness. But because we have an ego, behaving cruelly, greedily, and selfishly is a potential within all of us. When we're identified with the ego and its drives and desires, we feel stressed-out, we suffer, and we often also cause suffering to others. When we aren't identified with the ego, we are naturally at peace and loving toward others.

The ego and its programming as well as other conditioning is experienced as the voice in our head—that ongoing mental commentary that we're all so familiar with. If we identify with and believe what the voice in our head tells us, we are often left feeling bad and stressed-out. This aspect of the mind is called the *egoic mind,* since it generally serves the ego.

We experience the egoic mind as thoughts that seem to be our own thoughts, although they're just our programming. We aren't responsible for these thoughts being there; we didn't choose them or put them there. They were given to us and are what make us human beings, as opposed to spiritual beings. The thoughts that run through our mind represent the human condition and also provide us with an identity as a particular individual: "I'm a vegetarian, not very bright, good at basketball, afraid of cats, fun-loving, always screwing up." Thoughts about who we are, how we feel, and what we like run through our mind nearly constantly. We tend to agree that these thoughts describe us and rarely question them.

The thoughts that run through our mind seem to be what is true about ourselves, life, and others, while these thoughts are actually just the programming we received and the conclusions we've come to. This programming includes our psychological conditioning, personality traits, beliefs, preferences, and what we've learned. Some of these thoughts are positive, some are neutral, and many are negative and untrue.

The voice in our head talks to us about any number of things, but primarily it does the following:

❖ Expresses judgments, comparisons, beliefs, opinions, likes, dislikes, fears, and desires;

❖ Replays the past;

❖ Ruminates, speculates, plans, and fantasizes about the future;

❖ Comments on whatever we're experiencing;

❖ Thinks about other people; and

❖ Thinks about how *I* am doing and how *my* life is going. In this way, the voice in our head creates our identity.

When we're absorbed in such thoughts, we aren't fully experiencing whatever we're experiencing in the here and now. We aren't present to our life. Being lost in thought is a very different experience and different state of consciousness from being present. Being lost in thought is like living in a virtual reality rather than in reality. This virtual reality is not a place of peace, but of stress and suffering to one degree or another.

We think we need such thoughts to survive and be happy, but as we will see, this is a mistaken assumption. It's only our programming that causes us to believe this. We are programmed to believe that our thoughts are ours and that they are important, necessary to our survival, and true.

This voice in our head, our egoic mind, is distinct from the more functional aspect of our mind that we use to do mental work, such as reading, planning, studying, and adding and subtracting. The big difference is that we experience the egoic mind as a mental voice, while the functional mind, our intellect, is not experienced as a voice. It doesn't speak to us like the egoic mind does. The more functional aspect of the mind is simply a tool that we use to perform mental tasks. When we're absorbed in these mental tasks, our egoic mind is silent, since the egoic mind and functional mind can't be engaged simultaneously. For example, we can't carry on an inner dialogue with ourselves and read at the same time.

The egoic mind, as we will see, is actually not functional. We could even say it is dysfunctional, since not only can we do without it, but we're better off without it. This may come as a shock; however, there are many who live happily and effectively without listening to the voice in their head.

The idea that we can live without paying attention to the egoic mind is a radical idea, but an idea whose time has come. It's time for humanity to wake up out of the lies, stress, hatred, and unhappiness created by the egoic mind. Once we see the truth about this aspect of the mind, it's possible to discover that life is lived more peacefully, happily, lovingly, and effectively from the core of our being, from the Stillness, from which all life comes.

C H A P T E R 1

How We Create Stress and How to Stop

Where Stress Comes From

The world is stressful—or is it? People feel stressed, but is the world creating stress? It's possible to be in this busy world, accomplish what we need to, and feel very little stress. So something else must be causing stress besides the world around us. In fact, it's something inside us: our thoughts.

Stress is usually a sign that we need to stop a moment and examine what we're saying to ourselves. It is often caused by a "should," a judgment, a fear, a worry, or some other negative thought. Being identified with our thoughts often causes stress because so many of the thoughts that run through our mind are negative and therefore stressful.

Negative thoughts, as I'm defining them, are thoughts that cause tension in our body and a sense of contraction. There isn't actually anything wrong with any of our thoughts or with having them; they're part of the human experience. But since we don't like how certain thoughts make us feel, we'll call them negative. We could also simply call them stressful, since they create stress.

For example, the thought "I'm going to be late," although not stressful by itself, tends to be followed by stressful thoughts, possibly about being bad for being late or about what might happen because of it. Such thoughts of self-criticism and worry make us feel contracted, and that contraction is one way that stress is experienced in the body.

Stress results from believing the negative stories that our egoic mind, the voice in our head, tells us about ourselves, life, others, the past, the present, or the future. The egoic mind doesn't just give us information; it puts a spin on it. That spin usually tells a story about what something, such as being late, will mean personally to *me* and *my* life. And then feelings are triggered. The egoic mind is not a neutral voice, but often a voice of fear, panic, judgment, blaming, and shaming.

The irony is that we think we need such thoughts to function when, in fact, they interfere with handling life and make whatever we're doing less enjoyable. For instance, if you think you're going to be late, you're likely to be rushing, imagining negative scenarios about arriving late, and feeling any number of feelings. Meanwhile, you're not giving your full attention to whatever you need to do to get there and get there safely. As a result, you're more likely to forget something or have an accident, and you surely won't arrive cool and collected.

Stress generally isn't caused by circumstances, such as being late, although it often coincides with some circumstance or event. Rather, stress comes from the egoic mind's negative interpretation of circumstances and the negative feelings that come from that interpretation. The egoic mind interprets and draws conclusions about facts and events. These conclusions are stories that the egoic mind makes up about facts and events, and these stories are usually stressful.

These spins on life nearly always leave us feeling bad, because the tales the ego spins tend to be negative. The ego has a fearful outlook and is not wise, so its stories aren't trustworthy or useful. The egoic mind is not a friend or a wise mentor. It doesn't help us or provide real solutions. Instead, it is the cause of human suffering.

The voice in our head takes on many different guises. Sometimes it seems like our own voice. At other times, it may scold us like a parent, joke with us like a friend, or tell us what to do like a boss. It often dialogues with us or with some other inner persona. When you take a good look at this voice, you see that it's made up of a menagerie of voices representing different personas, or subpersonalities. These voices often argue with or contradict each other. They're quick to give advice but have little wisdom.

The voice in our head is often confused, fearful, doubting, complaining, resistant, demeaning, argumentative, bullying, and judgmental, which is one reason it's difficult to be a human being. We all carry around with us troublesome and trouble-making voices, which speak to us incessantly. If you had a friend who spoke to you like the voice in your head does, he or she probably wouldn't be your friend for long. And yet, we identify with this voice, that is, we agree with it, believe it, and even give it a voice. In fact, it becomes *our* voice (and then the problems begin!). We do this because we're programmed to do this.

Although the egoic mind often seems like your own voice, like what you think and believe, this voice is only masquerading as you. It isn't actually you or your voice but the programming you were given. It represents the conditioned self, not our true self. We are programmed to get our sense of self from our thoughts and to believe that our thoughts are who we are.

However, in reality, we are what is aware of the thoughts that run through our mind. We are what is conscious of our thoughts and of everything else we experience. This awareness, or consciousness, is the constant in your life, while all of your thoughts, feelings, self-images, sensations, experiences, and everything else in life come and go. Awareness is even constant in sleep, since you are always aware that you slept.

This awareness is often referred to simply as Awareness. Other names for it are Consciousness, Essence, the authentic self, the Self, Silence, Stillness, the Observer, the Watcher, or the Witness. Of course, there are many other names for it as well. I sometimes call it the Noticer, although it's more than just a noticer of life, as it is who we are and therefore life itself as it moves through us.

To be clear, Awareness is not the commentator that we hear in our mind, which may seem like an observer, as it notes what's happening moment to moment: "The mail isn't here yet. It's really windy today. I'm hungry." Awareness is what notices the commentary of the egoic mind and everything else. Awareness doesn't describe or note what it's aware of like the egoic mind does. Awareness is silent.

Awareness, who we are, can become so focused on an object, such as a thought, feeling, or self-image, that we lose the sense of being the witness of those things. Awareness often gets lost in, or identified with, what it's aware of or focused on. It zooms in on one small aspect of experience, and then we forget that we are Awareness. We become *identified* with the object that we are aware of. Temporarily, it feels like we *are* the object of our focus rather than what is aware of the object.

For example, if Awareness focuses on a feeling of sadness, you become sad and even identify yourself as sad: "I'm sad." Or if you focus on the pain in the finger you just cut, it seems like all that exists is that pain. Then if you focus on some other sensation, that pain can seem to disappear, as your attention gets lost in a new sensation, that is, until you pay attention to your finger again. When Awareness is focused so narrowly, it loses track of everything else that's going on. This is what happens when we get lost in thought: Our thoughts become our reality, and the rest of reality drops into the background.

But Awareness can never really be lost in any object of focus. Although it constantly moves in and out of identification with objects, Awareness hasn't gone anywhere. It's always here, aware of whatever it's aware of. All we have to do is notice what is aware of whatever we are focused on, and we'll zoom out and become identified with Awareness instead. For instance, if you notice what is aware of the pain in your finger, you'll regain your perspective on it: The pain in your finger is just one of many sensations in your awareness.

Spiritual evolution is about re-discovering, or realizing, ourselves as Awareness through dis-identification with the thoughts, feelings, self-images, and physical body that Awareness has identified with. This identification creates the false self, the sense that we are something other than Awareness, that we are an individual with a particular identity.

This distinction between Awareness, or the true self, and a programmed, or false, self is important because the false self, or ego, is the generator of all stressful thoughts. The ego—not the true self—is what is behind the voice in your head and any self-generated stress you experience. The true self, on the other hand, is the source of peace, wisdom, and love. (Isn't it great that our true nature is peace, wisdom, and love?) Our true self doesn't have a voice like the ego has but is experienced in the stillness in between our thoughts, which is why our true self is often simply called Stillness. It is pure, quiet, clear, and empty, like a motionless pool of water.

So, what does your mind tell you that makes you feel stressed? Maybe it tells you that you aren't good enough. Maybe it tells you that you aren't doing something fast enough. Maybe it lists all the things you still have left to do. Maybe it tells you that someone doesn't like you. Maybe it goes over how much you have in your bank account or how your stocks are doing. Maybe it reminds you of something someone did in the past. Maybe it imagines a terrible future. The list of possible stressful thoughts is endless, and we aren't conscious of many of them.

Take a moment, if you will, to ponder the things your egoic mind most often says that cause you to feel stressed and unhappy. You might want to write them down and add to this list as you become more aware of them. Everyone's egoic mind has certain favorite "tunes" it plays repeatedly. What plays most often on the radio station of your mind that causes you to feel stressed? Is it the "Hurry Up" song, the "There's Never Enough Time" song, the "I'm Not Happy" song, the "Everything's Terrible" song, the "I'm Not Good Enough" song, or the "It Shouldn't Have Happened" song?

Notice the relentlessness of some of the mind's messages. It repeats the same thoughts again and again. A small fraction of the thoughts we think each day are new. Most of our thoughts are the same thoughts day after day. So how useful can they be?

The egoic mind's radio station is undoubtedly one you would turn off if you could. Since you can't turn off this commentary, what can you do? You can turn down the volume, and that will make this voice easier to detach from and less bothersome. Awareness of this commentary is the first step in turning the volume down. Become aware of the commentary and recognize it for what it is—the egoic mind's chatter. And notice that it doesn't serve you. That realization will help you detach from it.

The next step in turning down the volume is to not give the egoic mind your attention. Instead, give your attention to whatever is happening, whatever you're experiencing through your senses, and whatever is arising within you that is truer and more positive than the mind's commentary, such as intuitions, insights, gratitude, wisdom, and inspiration.

The antidote to stress is changing the channel we are tuned to. When we are tuned in to Stillness instead of our egoic mind, we feel expansive and happy rather than contracted, unhappy, and stressed. When given a chance—when not drowned out by our mind's chatter—our beautiful being can be experienced, and it's experienced as peace, joy, compassion, gratitude, acceptance, wisdom, strength, and love.

Stillness's channel expands us rather than contracts us. It broadcasts signals and messages that guide us in directions that make us happy and fulfilled. It also broadcasts positive feelings, such as peace, love, gratitude, compassion, acceptance, and encouragement, which can counteract the mind's negative thoughts and the feelings that arise from those thoughts. We know when we're tuned in to Stillness because we feel relaxed, at peace, content, and accepting instead of stressed. So why stay tuned to The Stress Channel when another one is available?

At first, Stillness's channel may not come in as clearly as the ego's because Stillness communicates more subtly and not as loudly as the ego. But as we get better at tuning in to Stillness, the signal gets stronger, and the egoic mind's chatter becomes weaker. The more we tune in to Stillness, the easier it becomes and the less compelling the egoic chatter is. We really do have a choice about what we listen to.

Stillness's channel can only be heard when we're present in the moment—when we're fully absorbed in whatever experience we're having, not in our thoughts. Being present means being attentive to our sensory experience: what we are seeing, smelling, hearing, tasting, and sensing in our body as well as sensing more subtly and intuitively. To tune in to Stillness, all we have to do is *be, experience, notice,* and *naturally respond* to what's arising in the moment.

To tune in to The Stress Channel, we just have to start believing our thoughts again. The good news is that we have control over our level of stress. Eliminating stress is mostly a matter of tuning out the negative (what causes us to contract), tuning in the positive (what causes us to expand and be at peace) and just being, experiencing, and dancing to that music instead of to the mind's chatter.

Stress may also be a sign that we aren't making choices that support our health, happiness, well-being, and fulfillment. The ego often pushes us toward goals that aren't ultimately fulfilling, ones that don't really fit for us but are driven by fear and a sense of lack and not being good enough. Or the ego might limit us by talking us out of pursuing goals and activities that would make our heart sing. When we aren't in touch with Stillness, we often make choices that leave us feeling stressed, exhausted, unhappy, and even depressed, and we might not pursue something we would love to do.

There are lots of reasons to tune out The Stress Channel and to tune in to Stillness. Stress is not only unpleasant and unproductive; it affects our health.

How Stress Affects the Body

Bruce H. Lipton, Ph.D., author of *The Biology of Belief,* in the audiobook *The Wisdom of Your Cells* (published by Sounds True), explains that when there is a threat to our safety, stress hormones are released, which activate the fight or flight response, and energy is directed away from the immune system and other systems that maintain the body. If stress continues for a long time, we become vulnerable to the bacteria and viruses that are naturally present in our system, which our immune system regularly fights off. This is why when we're under stress we're more likely to become sick. Stress also interferes with cell repair, which can eventually compromise the functioning of the body's systems.

The other problem with stress is that it causes us to react reflexively rather than consciously and rationally. This is because stress deactivates the forebrain, or cerebral cortex, which is the seat of awareness, attention, sensory experience, and decision-making, and activates the hindbrain, the reflexive part of our brain. This means that when we're under stress, we become less intelligent and more reactive.

I can give an example of this in my own life. One day, in the middle of the afternoon, I stepped out on our deck and saw a huge plume of smoke. At the time, we lived in Prescott, Arizona on the edge of a pine forest. I called to my husband to come and look. We immediately realized that we had to evacuate because we not only saw smoke but flames. I tried to think of what to take, but my brain wouldn't work. I moved about as if in a trance. Fortunately, my husband's brain was working, and he gave me some instructions. When we arrived at my brother's house in Scottsdale, where we planned to stay until we could return home, I discovered I'd forgotten to pack my underwear!

Although most of us aren't faced with physical threats on a daily basis, as our ancestors were, our body's stress response is still very active, since it's triggered even when we don't need it by stressful thoughts. Under these circumstances, the stress response is actually dysfunctional because it wears down our body and makes us less rational rather than improving our ability to survive. So our imagined fears and other stressful thoughts do not actually have survival value, as we might think.

The Stress Channel

The Stress Channel is the ego's channel. When we're tuned in to the egoic mind and absorbed in our thoughts about ourselves and our life, we are tuned in to the ego. The reason this is stressful is that The Stress Channel broadcasts fear and a sense of lack, of not having or being enough. The ego produces the fear and discontentment and the sense of being separate and lacking that exemplifies the human condition. All humans are programmed with similar thoughts, and many of those thoughts lead to suffering to one extent or another.

We're going to look more closely at what is usually playing on The Stress Channel so that you can more easily recognize the thoughts produced by the ego. The more you're able to recognize the ego in your thoughts, the easier it will be to detach from those thoughts.

The really good news is that suffering is optional because, although we are in a human package, we are not actually human, but Spirit in a human disguise. This recognition, or realization, greatly diminishes the stress of being human. Once we stop believing what the mind is saying, the mind loses its power to make us suffer. Once you've seen through this voice, what it's saying no longer matters.

To be happy, this voice doesn't have to go away or even become more positive. The way out of suffering is not to change the egoic mind, which is difficult to do, but to simply recognize what it's up to and not buy into it. In the interest of doing that, let's take a look at some of the features of the egoic mind.

Thoughts Seem Like Ours

One of the features of this voice in our head is that it seems like our very own voice. That is the first illusion to be seen through. Just take a moment to do some inquiry:

❖ *Where do your thoughts come from?*

❖ *Can you find a you that these thoughts are happening to? They're happening within your body-mind, but are you your body-mind?*

❖ *Are your thoughts ones you'd like to have?*

❖ *Who is it that likes or doesn't like these thoughts?*

❖ *How can your thoughts be your own voice when you don't even like much of what this voice says and when, in fact, this voice often makes you feel bad?*

❖ *Who is it that is aware of not liking some of your thoughts?*

This voice in your head is not your voice, and it doesn't have to be your voice. You are what can choose to believe those thoughts and give voice to them and act on them or not. What is it that is aware of your thoughts and can choose this? This is a great mystery, isn't it? We are all a great mystery and part of an even greater Mystery.

Thoughts Seem True

The second illusion is that our thoughts seem true. We are programmed to automatically accept our thoughts without questioning them. But are they true? When we become more aware of our thoughts, we discover that many of our assumptions and beliefs are contradictory or untrue. They may have been true once, but are they true now?

Many of our beliefs are what we were taught as children. We accepted what we were taught then, often without questioning. As adults, most of us still don't question our beliefs because most of us aren't aware of what we are thinking. Racial prejudice is an example of beliefs that are acquired from others that shape our behavior until we examine them more closely.

As children and even more recently, we came to conclusions about ourselves, other people, life, and God based on our experiences and limited understanding. These conclusions become part of our identity and self-image and are reflected in the thoughts that run through our mind. Until we become more aware of these thoughts and examine them, we continue to believe them, and they determine our behavior and experience of life.

For example, if your father left your mother when you were young, you might have concluded that he didn't love you, that you were the reason your parents divorced, that men can't be trusted, that you'll never be happy, or any number of other understandable but false conclusions. These conclusions determine how you feel about yourself and others and therefore how you interact with others.

We automatically believe our thoughts, beliefs, assumptions, conclusions, and desires and let them guide our behavior. But how has that worked for you? Since what the egoic mind says and what it drives us to do is inconsistent and often contradictory or untrue, when we listen to it, we are left confused and constantly changing our mind or following a course that is unfulfilling. For true guidance, we have to turn to something deeper than our egoic mind.

Thoughts Seem More Important Than They Are

Another illusion is that our thoughts seem important. Notice how much more important your thoughts seem than they actually are. They have a weight about them that captures our attention. This is one of the ways the egoic mind keeps us involved with it, by making thoughts seem very important, as if we *must* pay attention to them to be safe and happy. But their importance is an illusion.

For example, how important is the thought "I need to remember to get milk"? If this thought didn't seem so important, then forgetting the milk wouldn't seem like such a big deal when it happens. We often get really mad at ourselves or others over relatively small things that go wrong. Why do these things seem so important? Important to whom? Many of the things that "go wrong" in our day, according to our egoic mind, are pretty minor—they just *seem* important at the time.

Our thoughts are, in a sense, magnified. And we take this magnification as the truth. We believe the level of importance our thoughts give to things. As you go about your day, just notice what your thoughts are saying about life and about what you "need" to do: "I have to do this" and "He has to do that (or else!)." We all have a mental list of what we'd like to accomplish and what we think we need to accomplish, but do you see that this list is arbitrary—made up? Who is it that says you have to do something? Is it you, or is it just a thought? Who is pushing you? Who is running the show? And how does that feel?

Most days are quite ordinary, filled with the usual, relatively unimportant tasks. But the mind makes even small tasks seem important. Our mind zooms in on the smallest things and blows them up out of proportion. It makes mountains out of molehills, as my mother used to say. This is just what minds do.

Are things as important as your mind tells you they are? Is it so terrible if things go differently than you thought? Is it so terrible if you forget something or make a mistake or someone else forgets something or makes a mistake? In any event, it is done, and there's no use crying over spilled milk (or no milk).

When things don't go as planned, simply asking, "Is it that important?" can be helpful. Answer this question from a place of being zoomed out: "Will this be important a year from now or several years from now? Will this be important on my deathbed?" Many of the things we get upset about wouldn't be important even moments or days later.

When the egoic mind doesn't have anything of real importance to focus on, it makes insignificant things important. The egoic mind makes life more serious and difficult than life needs to be. It makes some things that aren't a matter of life and death seem like they are. This is one of the ways that we (our egos) make ourselves important: If what we're doing is important, that means we are important.

Thoughts Tell Stories

This brings us to another feature of the egoic mind: It creates a sense of being someone by telling stories. The egoic mind is all about building and sustaining a sense of self, whether it's a positive sense of self or a negative one. One of the ways it does this is by making what we do and what happens to us a reflection of either our worthiness or unworthiness.

Throughout our day, the egoic mind refers experiences, even the most mundane ones, back to *me* and tells a positive or negative story about *me*. The ego examines each experience for what it might mean about *me* and comes up with conclusions, or stories. So even something like rain happening on the day you've planned a picnic becomes all about you: "Why does it always rain when *I* have something planned?" Or the ego puffs itself up by taking credit for something: "*I* manifested it," rather than recognizing all the forces at work that allowed that to come into manifestation.

Life is just the way it is, while the mind tells stories about how that relates to *me*. When we make a mistake, we declare: "I never do anything right." When we don't sleep well, we conclude: "I'm going to be off all day." When we spill something on our shirt, we call ourselves names: "I'm such a slob." Making a mistake, not sleeping well, and spilling things are common occurrences for everyone, but our egoic mind makes them mean something about us personally, usually something negative.

One of the main ways we create stress is by telling stories about events, when events are just events. Something happened. Period. What if we just let that be the way it is? Notice the tales the egoic mind tells. It is a liar—it makes up stories. Once you know someone is a liar, do you keep believing that person? Recognizing what the egoic mind is up to and how its stories make us feel stressed and unhappy releases us from the ego's grip. Seeing this is *not* believing!

The antidote to the stress and suffering caused by the egoic mind is letting everything be as it is. A mistake happens—let that be as it is (because it is). You forgot something—let that be as it is. You spilled something—let that be as it is. You lost $100,000 in the stock market—let that be as it is, without telling a story about it. It happened. Period.

Any story that we add on top of what simply happened doesn't change a thing. All our stories do is put a spin on what happened, which usually results in stress and unhappiness. Why bother? The ego bothers because telling stories is how it maintains the sense we have of being somebody who is lacking and at war with life. Telling stories is how the ego is maintained. But you are not the ego. You are not the voice in your head, so you don't have to agree with its rendition of life.

Thoughts Tell a Story of Lack

This brings us to another feature of the ego, which is a sense of lack. We are programmed to focus on what's missing and to overlook or minimize what *is* here. It's the old glass-is-half-empty syndrome. From the standpoint of the ego, you are never good enough, life is never good enough, and other people are never good enough.

We can't change this programming, but the more aware we are of it, the less power it has to affect how we see life. We can learn to see life through other than the ego's eyes. How does it feel to be lacking, for life to be lacking, for others to be lacking? Much of our stress comes from feeling this sense of lack, particularly a sense of lack within us.

The feeling of unworthiness or that something is missing in our life is often at the root of excessive busy-ness and striving and therefore at the root of stress. By being very busy or working very hard, we often try to compensate for such feelings of lack. Alternately, we might seek love and approval from others or compulsively try to fix and improve ourselves.

If these strategies don't work or if they've left us exhausted, we might turn to drugs, alcohol, or food to escape from our pain or to comfort or numb ourselves. Is it any wonder that addiction and overeating are major issues in our overly busy and stressed-out society? These are ways we're trying to take care of our exhausted, stressed-out selves. Unfortunately, these coping mechanisms don't work for long and leave us less healthy and feeling even worse about ourselves.

We need to get to the root of our busy-ness and stress, which is the sense of never being or having enough, which we all have to one extent or another by virtue of being human and having an ego. One of the antidotes to this sense of lack is to have compassion for the suffering caused by the dilemma of having an ego that is never satisfied. Summoning compassion for ourselves moves us out of the ego's domain and into Stillness, where it is possible to discover that nothing is lacking.

Thoughts Generate Desires

Another feature of the egoic mind is desires, most of which stem from the ego's fears and sense of lack. The ego believes that getting what it desires will quell its fears and sense of lack. The ego desires material things, but it also desires many intangible things, such as success.

Success, like so much of what the ego desires, is a concept, an idea. The trouble with desiring something as intangible as success is that such concepts are unattainable. As soon as the ego's idea of success is achieved, it changes its definition of success and sets another goal to strive and suffer over. As a result, success and every other concept that the ego strives for, such as beauty, recognition, status, security, and admiration, remain elusive and just out of reach. None of these will ever be achieved by the ego, at least not for long, because the ego continually redefines what that would mean. It is forever chasing after dreams, and that will never change, because it is the ego's nature to do this.

We, as humans, are programmed with similar egoic desires, although we also have deeper desires that are not egoic. We all desire possessions, security, comfort, safety, money, power, prestige, beauty, admiration, recognition, and success. Driving these egoic desires is the belief that we need these things to be happy. This is the lie that makes the world go round.

It's easy enough to see that this is a lie whenever we do finally achieve what we thought would make us happy, only to discover that other desires quickly take the place of the one that was fulfilled. Chasing after what we want only results in more wanting, not in satiation. This is because the ego is in the business of manufacturing desires, not peace and happiness. The ego is never satisfied for long or it would be out of business.

Getting off this unending wheel of desire requires seeing the truth about desire. There are actually many truths that need to be seen. One of them, which was just mentioned, is that fulfilling our desires leads to more desires, not satisfaction or lasting happiness.

Another truth is that desire, like every other thought, is fed by our attention and disappears without our attention. Have you ever longed for something very deeply, and then you forgot about it completely because another desire captured your attention? Desires are strengthened and maintained by our attention. If you want to be without the pain and stress of desiring, then stop thinking about what you desire. Focus on something else, preferably on your present moment experience, where true peace and happiness lie.

And finally, another truth is that our desires are not what ultimately shape life. Wanting something doesn't cause it to manifest. In fact, when we are dissatisfied, stressed-out, and unhappy because we want things to be different, we're less likely to get what we want than when we are content, because this negative state saps our energy and is not attractive.

Contentment, on the other hand, is an extremely attractive state. Contentment makes space for and draws to us what life intends for us. Notice I said "what life intends for us," not what we want, because sometimes what we want is not what life intends for us. There's a higher order in life than our desires. The Whole operates in support of the Whole. We can trust it to bring us the experiences we need that will ultimately benefit us and the Whole. Sometimes that experience is limitation, and sometimes it is abundance.

Experiences of limitation are an opportunity to develop our resources and talents as well as our inner strength, courage, patience, perseverance, and other virtues. Limitation can move us out of the superficial world of the ego, turn us inward, and make us a better human being. Getting what we want isn't always a good thing for our soul, our life's purpose, or the Whole.

Every experience we have is the right experience. The ego tries to make life go its way, but that's an impossible task and causes a lot of suffering and stress. Life will have its way with us. We have to learn to say yes to that even when the ego is screaming, "No!"

There are deeper, more meaningful desires that spur us on toward our life's purpose and the intentions of the Whole. These deeper desires aren't experienced in the same way as egoic desires, which are experienced as thoughts that develop into feelings of longing, frustration, and discontent. Deeper desires don't cause suffering, unless the mind gets hold of them. These deeper desires are experienced as drives that move us forward in personally meaningful directions. We are propelled by joy by these deeper desires to fulfill our life's purpose.

Thoughts Push Us to Strive and Hurry

Perhaps the most stressful feature of the egoic mind, which also stems from a sense of lack, is its tendency to push and hurry us. The ego is a time-tyrant and a judge. We can never do things fast enough or well enough for it. The more we listen to this voice that pushes and hurries us, the more stressed-out we feel and the less satisfaction and joy we get from whatever we're doing.

Listening to this voice often leads to multitasking. By multitasking, the ego is trying to get a lot done at once, usually so that it can get on to something else. But there's no end to the ego's to-do list! The ego pushes us to do more and more and to get whatever we're doing done as soon as possible. Life becomes a race to the finish, but there's no finish line.

What is it that feels that there isn't enough time? Is that really true? And how is it to feel this way? The ego, of course, is what pushes us to try to squeeze more and more into every day. It often does this with fear: "Something terrible will happen if you don't get it all done!" Or the voice might promise a reward: "When you get it done, you can relax and be happy (but not before then)." Whether the mind prods us with fear or with the hope of happiness, success, approval, or something else, this voice is one of the main causes of stress.

The truth is, we can only give our attention fully to one thing at a time. So how stressful can that be? It's easy to do one thing at a time, no matter what it is. Even if it's brain surgery, we're only making one movement at a time. What makes doing something difficult and stressful is worrying about what needs to be done, trying to conform to the ego's arbitrary deadlines, and trying to do too many things at once.

Multitasking has become an accepted — and expected — way of operating, particularly in business. However, since the mind can only attend fully to one thing at a time, moving back and forth between a number of tasks, or even just two, isn't necessarily more efficient and often results in mistakes or a job that isn't as well done as it might have been.

Even when multitasking is more efficient (and there are times when it is), is the stress involved in trying to keep track of a number of things at once and trying to get them done quickly worth it? The next time you're hurrying or multitasking, notice how your body feels. Our bodies tense up when we hurry or try to do too much at once. This tension is often expressed as anger, such as road rage, crankiness, or complaining. Stress puts our body into fight or flight. This explains why anger, which is a fighting response, is so common when we feel stressed.

What's more important—getting things done as fast as you can or experiencing what you're doing and enjoying it while you're doing it? The trouble with doing a number of things at once is that we usually aren't fully present to any one of them. Instead, we're hurrying and not enjoying ourselves. But when we slow down and are fully present to what we're doing, a natural enjoyment arises. And perhaps more importantly, wisdom about how to do whatever we're doing and even whether it's worth doing has a chance to register within us. When we slow down, we make space for our own inherent wisdom to arise and take charge of the activity.

When we allow the egoic mind to run our activities, we end up feeling like a machine: soul-less and joyless. You can be a machine if you want, but is that how you want to live your life? There's another choice (even if you think there isn't), and that is to slow down, be present, notice what's arising to be done, do it, and move on to the next thing. And sometimes, amidst all the doing, stop, check inside, and just let yourself be. Take in the glory of life as if there were nothing more to do. We often let ourselves do this after we've completed something, but why not do this more often?

A slower-paced lifestyle isn't in keeping with the business model, but the business model is no way to run our lives. The business model isn't even healthy for the corporations themselves. Nor is it healthy for our society. It's obvious what the corporate mentality has done to our environment. When profit is the primary goal, then the rest of life isn't sufficiently honored. When we allow the egoic mind to be our master, we lose our soul, our juice, our *joie de vivre*. Multitasking is often the result of an egoic mind that's been allowed to run amok, a mind that is driven by fear, lack, and desire.

The antidote to a mind that has run amok is noticing the result of multitasking on your body and your spirit. How do you feel when you're multitasking? If you're contracted, stressed, or unhappy because of how you're doing things, then stop and do only one thing at a time. Multitask only when you can do it with joy and without feeling stressed, which will probably require slowing down.

When you're doing something, check how you're feeling and then modify how you're doing it until you are enjoying it. You don't have to be a slave to your egoic mind or to other people's. Once you realize the need for change, you can change how you do things.

You deserve peace and happiness. Doing is not more important than being and everything that comes with being: love, peace, and joy. How can you modify how you perform your responsibilities to make them more of a joy than a burden? Here are some suggestions:

❖ Instead of immediately jumping into the next task when you finish something, stop for a few moments, take a few deep breaths or do something else to bring yourself into the present moment. Specific suggestions for becoming more present are offered in the fourth chapter.

❖ Slow down. Moving quickly tends to make us feel hurried and makes us more prone to mistakes. Slowing down is the antidote to the egoic mind's "hurry up." Slowing down puts you back in the flow and out of the ego's control.

❖ Give your full attention to whatever you are doing. As the Zen saying goes: "When you eat, just eat." Even when we aren't multitasking, we're often thinking about something else, which is in a sense multitasking. When you're doing something, notice your thoughts but don't get lost in them. Be in your body and senses instead of your head, and give your attention to whatever you're doing or whatever's happening in your environment.

Thoughts Create a Virtual Reality

Another feature of the egoic mind is that it creates a virtual reality of sorts. How believable our thoughts are! They create an illusory world that we live in, more or less. Those who spend less time in this illusory world feel freer, happier, more content, and more alive and open to life's possibilities. This illusory world is not a happy place but the source of all suffering.

Even discovering that some of the thoughts in your mind aren't true is a very big step to becoming free of this illusory world. From there, the illusion unravels further. Ultimately you discover that none of your thoughts about yourself—or about anyone or anything else—are true! That's pretty radical. The truth is radical. It's radical to discover that you don't need the voice in your head to guide your life or to be safe and happy. The truth is quite the opposite: Believing that voice takes you out of reality, where happiness, peace, fulfillment, and guidance are available.

Our thoughts aren't true because they can never match or describe reality fully enough. They are never the whole truth. They leave out so much. Besides, our ideas are just our particular spin, our particular perspective. For instance, if you describe someone, you're only describing a few of that person's characteristics, based on your perception of that person from past experience. Each of us is a complex and ever-changing mystery that can't be captured by a few labels. And every moment is a new moment. Who knows what someone is like right now?

Reality is what we know to be true and real right here and now. No self-image or story that you tell can match what is real and true right now. Is an image or a belief about yourself, someone else, or life true right now? Is it the whole truth? When you begin to examine your thoughts this thoroughly, you discover that they don't match reality. When your thoughts don't match reality, that's a recipe for suffering. For example, if you think that your husband should buy you flowers on your anniversary and he doesn't, you'll probably feel bad.

We all carry around both conscious and unconscious images of ourselves that shape how we respond to life. When we identify with one of our self-images, we behave accordingly. We bring that self-image to life and make it true for the time being. For instance, one of my self-images is that of a complainer. If in a particular moment I believe that I am that self-image, then I'll probably complain. On the other hand, if I notice this self-image coming to the forefront but don't identify with it, then I probably won't complain. In this way, our ideas about ourselves color our experience of reality and contribute to shaping it. Meanwhile, who we really are is here in the midst of this enacting of our self-images.

What would life be like if you didn't color reality this way with your self-images and beliefs? Once we drop out of our thoughts about ourselves and are just here, stripped bare of these ideas, we see that reality is waiting for us to discover it. What we find is that reality is sweet—and mysterious—and so are we.

How can any image, idea, or story match reality, when reality is constantly changing? We humans are concept-makers. Our mind makes up concepts, and these concepts help us communicate with others and function in society. But concepts don't describe or do justice to reality nor to the mysterious reality that we are. Concepts define and limit reality.

So what's reality like right now? What are you like right now? What do you actually know? A self-image may be present, but what else is present that is much bigger and truer than any self-image?

It's really good news that we are not our self-images, our beliefs, our past, our desires, or our future dreams! You are too mysterious and vast to be so narrowly defined. Let yourself be as vast as you truly are. Let yourself discover who you are beyond all self-images, beliefs, opinions, likes, dislikes, and desires.

Thoughts Don't Accept Reality

Another feature of the ego is that it wants life on its own terms. The ego doesn't actually like life or accept reality as it is. The ease with which the ego finds fault with things is part of our survival mechanism, but it causes us a great deal of distress and stress. If nothing is ever right, how can that not feel stressful? And if nothing is ever right, then naturally we would struggle against life to make it right.

One of the things that isn't right about reality, from the ego's viewpoint, is the fact that everyone ages and passes away. Instead of accepting this fact, the ego argues with reality: "I shouldn't have all these wrinkles. He shouldn't have died."

Arguing with the way things are is futile and only results in negative emotional states, which are painful, stressful, and take their toll on the body.

The ego also argues with the fact that everything changes. Change is unstoppable and inevitable. Often it can't even be slowed down. Nothing has ever stayed the same, so to assume that something or someone shouldn't change is useless. Everything on this planet is in a state of change and evolution. The ego sees this as bad. But the truth is that all this change is just as it's meant to be. Even if you don't believe that, seeing it otherwise only makes you stressed-out, unhappy, and disappointed.

There is a constant flow in each of our lives that brings us new perspectives, new ideas, and new ways of being. We can influence that flow, but we can't change or stop the flow itself. Trying to do so only results in unhappiness and stress. The best we can do is to go with the flow of life, make the best of it, and play the part we're meant to play in it. To resist the flow is to go against life, to go against reality.

This doesn't stop our egoic mind from not liking something or from railing against it, because our mind's job is to reject reality. Our mind was built to do that. Fortunately, we aren't our mind but something else, which is able to choose to accept reality and go with the flow of life instead of resist it. We can say no to the mind's arguments with reality and yes to the way things are showing up in a particular moment. Doing anything other than that creates tension in our bodies and emotions that we don't want to have, and that's stressful.

Our emotions are another aspect of reality that the ego doesn't like. The ego wants to feel good constantly. It imagines a life in which this would be the case and strives to make life be that way. But good feelings, like everything else, come and go. If we want to avoid suffering, we need to accept the appearance and disappearance of the various emotional states.

Emotions are part of being human. Like the weather, they move in and they move out. To say no to an emotion is like saying no to a cloud or no to the rain. If an emotion is present, we might as well let it to be there and find out about it. Being present means being curious about everything that's showing up in our present moment experience, not only the things we like, but also emotions we may not like.

The irony is that the ego is responsible for our unpleasant emotions *and* it rejects these emotions. Our emotions are for the most part caused by believing what the mind says. The ego is behind most of our negative emotional states and then it rails against them! Fortunately, we aren't these states nor the ego that created them, so once we realize this, we can be free of much of the suffering and stress caused by our ego and its rejection of our emotions.

There's a way out of the suffering caused by having an ego, a way out of the human condition. The way out isn't to reject or fight with the ego, our emotions, or reality but to accept and befriend these things. The way out is to transform our relationship to them to a more friendly one. We can become free of suffering if we can learn to accept the ego and our feelings and have compassion for ourselves and the human condition. What heals emotions is accepting that they are part of the human experience while realizing that our true nature is divine and not human. Much more will be said about this in the third chapter.

Another aspect of reality that the ego doesn't accept is difficulties. The ego wants and believes it should have no difficulties. Tires shouldn't get flat, teeth shouldn't get cavities, bosses should always be amiable, spouses should always love you, children should always be well behaved, and accidents should never happen. But these difficulties are part of everyone's life.

We often take difficulties personally and blame ourselves for occurrences that are a normal part of life: "If I were more lovable, my spouse would always treat me well. If I were a better mother, my children would always be well behaved. If I weren't so clumsy, I wouldn't have any accidents." These are the kinds of lies we tell ourselves, which make us feel bad whenever something challenging happens. We turn on ourselves by telling a negative story rather than just accepting that this is the way life is showing up right now.

No one escapes challenges. They are neither good nor bad; they just *are*. Notice how your egoic mind often turns challenges into a story that leaves you feeling victimized, angry, or bad about yourself. These stories are stressful. This is stress we create and therefore stress we can learn to not create. Events don't have to be stressful. It's the stories we tell about them that make them so.

Thoughts Judge and Compare

Another feature of the ego is that it judges and compares. This seems to be one of the ego's main jobs, as this tendency is so prevalent. Have you noticed how instantly the egoic mind comes up with a judgment or comparison, often based on very little knowledge about someone or something?

Many of our stories are made up of such judgments and comparisons: "We broke up because he wasn't good enough for me" instead of just "We broke up." Notice how most of the ego's judgments, comparisons, and stories make you feel bad. And the ones that make you feel good are often at the expense of others, where you assume that you're better than someone else. Much of the commentary that runs through our mind is of this nature.

Judgments make the ego feel safer because they give the ego a sense of knowing something, even if the judgment is incorrect. The ego would rather form an immediate and incorrect judgment than have none at all because the ego doesn't like not knowing. This distaste for not knowing drives the ego to draw conclusions and form opinions about something with very little knowledge about it.

Notice how quickly your mind comes up with a judgment. The beauty is that in noticing this, we're no longer at the mercy of that judgment. I say "mercy" because judgments don't feel good. They contract us, and they are rarely functional. Judgments are a way the ego pretends to know something and attempts to be on top (or on the bottom if the ego is trying to uphold a negative self-image).

Judgments aren't what they're cracked up to be. They don't actually come from a place of wisdom and discrimination but from the egoic mind, which is not wise, only conditioned. The egoic mind is conditioned with a lot of lies, half-truths, and prejudices, which makes what it says of questionable value. Wisdom, on the other hand, comes from our true self, and discrimination comes from our intellect. The egoic mind is neither our true self nor our intellect.

The ego's comparisons aren't valuable either. Like judgments, comparisons serve the ego's desire to be one up or one down. Comparisons don't serve us or life. What purpose does comparing yourself to others serve when we're all so unique? If apples can't be compared to oranges, then one person certainly can't be compared to another. Someone might be better at doing something than someone else, but that doesn't make that person better or worse than someone else, which is the implication when we compare someone to another.

The mind's tendency to compare ourselves with others isn't useful. The way you can know this is by how you feel when you do this—it contracts you. The mind's comparisons are harmful and limiting to us and to our relationships. Once you see this, you can be free of doing this. Throwing out your ego's comparisons doesn't mean you won't be discriminating in picking fruit or choosing a new car or a partner. Discrimination is a function of our intellect, not our egoic mind.

We don't have to identify with, that is, believe and agree with, the judgments and comparisons that run through our mind. Thinking such thoughts is just what the mind does. These thoughts aren't unique to you, they aren't wise, and they don't serve you or anyone else. Given this, judging ourselves for judging also doesn't serve. That's just more ego doing what it does.

To be free of the stress caused by judgments,
all you need to do is:

1. Notice and identify any judgments that are running through your mind, including any judgments about having judgments,

2. Accept those judgments as part of the human condition, and

3. Move your attention elsewhere, onto your real experience in the here and now.

How to Create Stress and How Not To

Below is a list to help you remember what to do and what not to do to have less stress in your life. The desire for less stress runs deeper than the ego's desires. This desire along with the desires for wholeness, peace, love, and happiness reflect our soul's desire to return to our true nature. Becoming less stressed is a way to do that. Stress keeps us involved with the ego, while a lack of stress allows us to drop into Stillness. Just in case you don't already know, here's how to create stress:

❖ As you go about your day, think about all the things you have to do. Go over your to-do list mentally many times a day, especially in the midst of doing something. Be sure to tell everyone how busy you are, how much you have to do, how exhausted you are, and how you'll never get it all done on time.

❖ Keep checking the time and think about time a lot: how much time something took, how much time something takes, how much time something will take, how much time you have left. Tell yourself that you don't have enough time or worry that you don't.

❖ Constantly judge and compare yourself with others: "Did I do that well enough? I should have done that better. Was it as good as last time? Was it as good as how Mom did it? How come he always does everything better than me?"

❖ Set a goal and make that more important than anything else. Imagine that you won't be happy until you achieve a particular goal and then push yourself harder than everyone else. Don't rest, don't enjoy what you're doing, don't take time for relationships, don't take time to eat right or exercise. Just keep your nose to the grindstone, no matter how you feel.

❖ Tell negative stories: "I can't do anything right. Life is too hard. No one will ever love me. I'll never be happy. Other people are jerks! She's never nice to me. Why is my life always so hard?" Be sure to include "always" and "never" in your stories to make them especially convincing.

❖ Want something other than what is. Wish and long to be different and for your life to be different. Be heartbroken that things aren't the way you want them to be. Dream of how your life could be or should be or how perfect other people's lives are. Then tell everybody how unhappy you are and what a failure your life is.

❖ Do it all. Believe that you should be able to do it all and do it all perfectly: everything you think you need to do, everything everyone else wants you to do, and everything you want to do. Assume that everyone else is juggling all these things perfectly.

❖ Don't take time to rest or do the things you'd really like to do or the things that mean the most to you. Say yes to every request from others. Make everyone else's needs more important than yours. Don't take care of yourself. Don't be kind to yourself. Don't make Stillness, relaxation, or enjoyment of life a priority.

❖ The good news is that all of this stress-creation is happening within your own mind, so you can do something about it. Here's how *not* to create stress:

❖ Don't listen to the mind's negativity, judgments, and comparisons. Notice what a liar, exaggerator, and fear-monger the mind is. Notice how its lies create feelings if you listen to it.

❖ Slow down so that you can smell the roses as you go. Don't listen to the "Hurry up" voice of the ego. Enjoy the ride. There really is time for everything, at least for everything that's really important.

❖ Do one thing at a time. Limit multitasking to things you can do easily and joyfully without creating stress.

❖ Don't set arbitrary timelines and deadlines for what you have to do. Be flexible about what you do and when and don't set deadlines for things that don't need deadlines. Allow things to get done more naturally, in their own time. The flow has a natural rhythm and grace in which things that need to get done do get done.

❖ Stop thinking about what you have to do. Making a to-do list can help the mind relax, but don't keep going over it mentally during your day. While you're doing other things, don't think about what else you have to do or plan to do or even want to do. Just be present to whatever you *are* doing.

❖ Notice what the egoic mind wants and then recognize that getting what it wants is not the source of happiness. The egoic mind always wants something other than what is. Give your attention to what *is* here, not to what isn't.

❖ Do what you do out of joy as it naturally arises to be done, not because your mind is pushing you to do it. Notice how the mind pushes you to do things, and don't listen to it. Instead, notice how your being is moving you and what it's naturally drawn to doing.

❖ Get really involved in whatever you are doing. Experience it fully with all of your senses. Be in the *experience* of the present moment and not lost in your thoughts.

❖ Don't say yes out of obligation. When you don't feel an inner yes, say no to others' requests for your help. Reserve some of your time and energy for things you love to do.

❖ Be kind to yourself. Let yourself and everyone else be imperfect. Expect mistakes. We will always be flawed and make mistakes. Sometimes, we will be less than stellar human beings. Forgive and have compassion for yourself and others. It's hard to be a human being!

❖ Do what brings you joy, peace, and love. Make love, peace, and happiness more important than things and more important than getting things done. You'll find that many of the things you think you need to do don't actually need to be done. They aren't as important as your mind thinks they are.

Letting Go of Your Mental Baggage

Our minds are so full! They are full of the past, full of the future, full of desires and fears, full of judgments, full of opinions, full of pain. These thoughts weigh heavily on us. We carry them around like baggage. Into each new moment, we bring these thoughts, and they color our experience or take us entirely out of this fresh, alive moment.

Many of us live inside our mental reality, our virtual reality, and very little in the reality of the present moment. This wouldn't be such a problem if this mental reality were a pleasant one. But our mental baggage tends to make us stressed-out and discontent with life. Our thoughts make life unpleasant. We may not even realize that life isn't actually unpleasant, only our baggage makes it so! How profound this realization is when this is really seen.

In moments when we experience life free of the spin that our thoughts put on it, what a relief it is! We all have moments like this, when we are so absorbed in whatever we're doing that we aren't thinking about ourselves. We're just being. When that happens, the sense of *me* falls away, and we experience being in the flow and responding naturally to life. We act and speak spontaneously without thinking and without evaluating those actions first. This is the natural state, and we're all familiar with it to some extent and experience it daily.

It's possible to live in the natural state most of the time. Only one thing is required: leaving your baggage behind. Did you realize that you could do that? We hang on to our mental baggage because we believe we need our thoughts. We do need our baggage to maintain a sense of being someone who has problems, needs, and desires, but we don't need our baggage to be alive and happy and to fulfill our life's purpose.

All that our baggage gives us is a false sense of self: a sense of ourselves as someone who feels and behaves a certain way and who has a certain history and certain dreams and desires for the future. Has this sense of yourself ever actually accomplished anything? Isn't it just thoughts about yourself? Do you really need such thoughts to exist and to function?

What's been living your life all along is here right now. It isn't dependent on your self-images or stories. These, after all, are just thoughts. They could be different, and you would still be alive. You would still exist. So obviously you aren't these thoughts, nor is being who you are dependent on them. The truth is, you don't need thoughts about yourself to exist or function. Most of the stories and images we have about ourselves interfere with our happiness and with fulfilling our potential. All we need our self-images and stories for is to uphold our self-images and stories, to uphold the false self.

It's absolutely safe to leave your self-images, stories, and the rest of your mental baggage behind. Life goes much better when we do, because our natural state is one of wisdom, love, kindness, peace, strength, and clarity. Our baggage interferes with everything we really want: love, peace, and happiness. You don't need your thoughts about yourself, about life, or about other people. You don't even need your desires, fears, judgments, or opinions. So you can stop bringing these thoughts into the present moment. Here's how to do that:

1. Notice the thoughts you're bringing to this moment. Is that thought a memory, a self-image, a worry, a fear, a belief, an opinion, a judgment, a desire, a fantasy?

2. Who is it that is able to notice these thoughts? You are what is able to notice your thoughts. Your thoughts only represent

the false self. Who you really are is what is aware of your thoughts and of everything else. This that you are is conscious of life, wise, loving, and happy to be alive.

When you stop believing that you are the one thinking the thoughts and realize that you are the one who is aware of the thoughts, you'll find true happiness and peace. The only thing preventing you from recognizing this is believing that you are the thinker instead of Awareness. Really let this sink in, because when you see that your thoughts have nothing to do with you, you'll be able to detach from them and they'll cease to affect your experience of life.

You drop your mental baggage because you see that it offers nothing of value but only takes you away from the experience of the beautiful being that you are.

Practices and Explorations

1. Practice being aware of your thoughts. Where do thoughts come from? Thoughts arise out of nowhere. Just because a thought is happening in your own head doesn't mean it's truer than a thought that is happening in someone else's head. What thoughts are showing up in your mind right now? Where did they come from? Someone? Something you read? Something you were taught? A TV commercial? Are they true? Are they wise? Are they useful in this moment? Are they helpful or destructive? How necessary are most of your thoughts? Do you need them to function? Do they help you function better or not? How do they make you feel?

2. As you go about your day, consider the possibility that the voice in your head and your thoughts about yourself don't belong to you or say anything true or meaningful about you.

They're just words that come out of nowhere, which happen to show up in your mind. Everyone has such thoughts, but they aren't important, valuable, or necessarily true. They're just a lot of chatter going on in the background of life. Meanwhile, you are alive, existing, and acting in each moment. That is what's real.

Stillness's Channel

We could just as well call this The Love Channel, The Happiness Channel, The Peace Channel as The Stillness Channel. What these names point to is our natural state. This channel is available anytime because our natural state is always here regardless of whether we are tuned in to it or not. That's why it's called the natural state.

On the other hand, The Stress Channel is our programmed, or default, state. Although it is most people's normal state, it's not the natural state. Humanity is evolving from the default state, or the egoic state of consciousness, to the natural state. Many people have already learned to do this, and this development is reflected in their brains, as neuroscience has demonstrated.

We have the power to be happy and at peace! We are not at the mercy of outer circumstances or our egoic mind. What a blessed time in history this is, that so many have already learned to shift out of the default state! The more people who learn to do this, the easier it will be for everyone else. What grace it is that there's a way out of suffering and we don't need to have the ego's desires met to be happy and at peace.

Happiness, peace, love, wisdom, clarity, compassion, acceptance, strength, patience, and curiosity are some of the qualities of our natural state. When we in touch with our true nature, we experience these qualities to one degree or another.

One of these qualities is often prominent for a time until another takes its place or we become identified with the ego again. Just as the egoic state of consciousness has certain features, our natural state has certain qualities.

When we're tuned in to Stillness, we know it because of how we feel. Stillness is a place of peace and no stress because Stillness is the experience of contentment and the sense that all is well and unfolding as it needs to. Stillness feels very full and complete, with nothing missing. Isn't this what we all want? In contrast, The Stress Channel is a place of fear and desire.

When we are in Stillness, the experience in our body and energy is aliveness, vibrancy, and peace. The stillness we experience when we are in Stillness is an inner stillness, not necessarily an outer stillness. A lot could be going on and we could be very busy. But when we are in Stillness, we experience an inner stillness, like being in the eye of a tornado or on a perfectly calm lake.

This inner stillness reflects another important quality of our true nature: It can't be harmed, affected, disturbed, or defiled by anything. It isn't affected by our negative emotions or harmful acts, by trauma or abuse, by events, by thoughts, or by any other experience that our body-mind might have. Our true nature is steady, receptive, and accepting of everything that happens, including our own misguided conclusions and behaviors. It welcomes everything about life and is unchanged by it. This ever-present, loving power at our core is who we really are.

We don't have to do or get anything to experience Stillness; all that's required is being present in the here and now—in reality. Peace, happiness, love, contentment, acceptance, wisdom, strength, and clarity come from giving attention to what's in front of us, from being very present to life as it is showing up.

Whenever we lose ourselves in whatever we're doing or in whatever's going on and are not preoccupied with thoughts but just experiencing whatever is happening, we feel happy, at peace, grateful, and connected to life in a way that feels like life is living us and we're just responding easily and naturally to it. This is our natural state. It is a state of *being* and of pure experiencing, although spontaneous actions also often arise out of it.

Being happy and at peace comes more from *not doing* certain things that obscure Stillness than from doing anything to get happiness and peace. The qualities of our true nature are revealed whenever we stop doing whatever tends to get in the way of experiencing Stillness.

The *only* thing that can interfere with experiencing Stillness is thoughts—about ourselves, our life, how it's all going, the past, the future, judgments, and other ideas. Such thoughts interfere with happiness and peace because they keep us in the egoic mind's virtual reality and from being fully engaged with life, with what's going on *now* in the flow of life.

When we're in the flow of life, we find our way to meaningful activities, or whatever we're doing is enjoyable and therefore meaningful. We feel moved internally by a force beyond us, like a river carrying us forward. We see beauty everywhere and feel immense gratitude and awe for life. That is how our true self experiences life. That is the experience of Stillness.

Practices

1. Take a few minutes to stop all doing and just sit and be quiet. Can you find the place within where nothing is moving, where you are still, content, and at peace, where *me* and *my life* and *what I have to do* don't exist? How do you experience

Stillness? Let the mind think what it thinks and let the body feel what it feels and just stay in the Stillness for a while. Throughout your day, you can stop a moment and do this. You are never too busy to take just a moment to check in with Stillness.

2. What are the occasions when you naturally and easily experience Stillness? When you're walking in nature? Just before you fully wake up or go to sleep? When you're playing or listening to music? When you look into the eyes of a child? When you're sitting by the water? Notice Stillness as it shows up, sometimes unexpectedly, in your day. The more you notice Stillness and spend time in it, the more it becomes part of your life. When you give your attention to Stillness, it deepens and opens up.

CHAPTER 2

Stressful Thoughts and Their Antidotes

Notice How Your Thoughts Make You Feel

Whatever thoughts we repeatedly give our attention to are strengthened and create an emotional climate, or state. This state becomes our experience of life for the time being until other thoughts and another state take their place. If things aren't going well for us on a particular day, we may be absorbed in thoughts of "poor me" or fears about what else might go wrong. These thoughts and feelings then color our experience of whatever else is going on that day. It may be a beautiful spring day, bursting with flowers, but we barely notice it. Our head is full of gloom instead of blooms.

In this way, we create our reality — our *experience* of reality, that is, and to some extent our actual reality. We are aware of gloom or blooms, depending on what we're giving our attention to: the mind or flowers. When we give our attention to our mind instead of the here and now, we experience life through the lens of our thoughts and feelings. This means that not only are we not experiencing life purely, but we're experiencing it in a distorted way, colored by the discontentment, fear, distrust, desires, and sense of lack of the ego.

Many of our moods and unpleasant emotions are the result of unconscious beliefs or thoughts that we aren't aware of. When that's the case, we just feel bad without knowing why. These feelings can be healed by letting them be there, accepting them, experiencing them, and then examining them to uncover the limiting beliefs that underlie them. More will be said about this in the next chapter.

Something that's a little easier to do than this and possibly an easier place to start in freeing yourself from stressful thoughts is to notice how the thoughts that you *are* aware of make you feel. Then ask yourself: "Does this thought make me feel relaxed, loving, and at peace with life or the opposite? Does it allow me to drop into Stillness or does it stir up emotions and keep me ensnared in the egoic state of consciousness?" It's important to examine the effect that your thoughts have on you and not just agree with them because they're happening in your body-mind. They may seem like your thoughts, but they have nothing to do with who you really are.

Rather than ignoring thoughts that make us feel bad, we often dwell on them, as if doing so has some benefit. Unfortunately, all this does is strengthen the mistaken belief, judgment, desire, or fear; make that thought more believable; and sustain the feelings. The more attention we give our thoughts, the more believable and emotion-packed they become.

Do negative thoughts and the feelings they generate, such as resentment, hatred, anger, jealousy, fear, worry, shame, guilt, or blame serve you? Do they serve life? Negative feelings not only feel bad, they also often make us act in ways that create more negative feelings for ourselves and others. Does acting out or even expressing such feelings serve you, serve others, or serve life? The result usually only adds to our collective pain as human beings.

Can we all agree that negative thoughts and their result, negative feelings, don't serve us? If you don't agree, then you might want to do some inquiry regarding what you believe about your negative thoughts to see if you can uncover the lies that keep you believing them and keep you creating negative feelings:

❖ *What do you believe about your negative thoughts?*

❖ *Do you believe they are wise and protective?*

❖ *Do you think they keep you safe? Safe from what?*

❖ *What are you afraid will happen if you stop giving your attention to your negative thoughts?*

Once we see that our negative feelings don't serve us, rejecting them, getting upset when they show up, or denying them is not the answer. If we do that, those feelings will keep returning and we'll miss the gift they have to offer us. The gift is that they point to a mistaken belief or misunderstanding. We can ask ourselves: "What did I just tell myself that made me feel this way?"

Negative emotions are red flags that show us that we're not in touch with the whole truth but with the ego's limited and limiting truth. The ego's perspective is generally self-centered, self-serving, and narrow, leaving out a bigger, truer perspective. The ego's perspective usually makes us feel bad if we agree with it. That's how we know it's the ego's perspective! The true perspective has the opposite effect.

Believing egoic thoughts causes so much unnecessary stress and unhappiness. To correct this, all we need to do is stop believing those thoughts, which is a matter of seeing that they aren't the whole truth. Once we see their falseness, we naturally stop believing them. Taking some time to investigate these thoughts will expose their falseness. This is something that may need to be done repeatedly if you continue to be taken in by a negative thought.

The more complete perspective is the perspective of our true self. We can discover this perspective when we are still. When we are in touch with Stillness's perspective, we feel at peace and in love with life. Then the goodness of life, of ourselves, and of others shines forth. Feeling this way is not only a benefit to ourselves but to others, because when we feel happy, we're kinder, wiser, and more effective than when we're unhappy. Our happiness allows others we touch to flourish as well. Our happiness is important. It helps the rest of the world be happy.

We can become adept at managing our emotional state by becoming more aware of our thoughts and their effect on us. Both cognitive therapy and mindfulness meditation recognize the role that awareness plays in reducing stress and emotional suffering.

Some of our thoughts are neutral, some are practical, but many are judgments, fears, desires, stories, beliefs, and other ideas that are part of our conditioning or the ego's perceptions and don't have any real value. All they do is make us feel stressed-out, dissatisfied, and inadequate.

We don't have to be victimized by our thoughts. Once we realize that thoughts that cause negative feelings come from the ego and have no value (yes — all of them!), we can choose to not get involved with them, to not add more fuel to them or give voice to them. This isn't always easy to do, but it does get easier the more we practice it. Isn't it great that we have the ability to free ourselves from the pain and stress of negative thoughts and emotions?

In the interest of being less at the mercy of stressful thoughts, what follows in the next sections are some key thoughts that will be helpful to become more aware of.

"I" Thoughts

Who would think that at the top of the list of stressful thoughts is the thought *I*? To be fair, *I* by itself doesn't necessarily cause us to contract. It might simply be referring to the most basic fact: *I exist.* It's what comes after *I* or *I am* that causes us to contract, because what usually follows is a narrow definition of ourselves, most likely some quality of our personality, our body-mind, a judgment, or a feeling. What comes after *I* or *I am* generally reflects the perspective of our false self and leaves out the experience of our true self. "I am old, I am lazy, I am tall, I'm not smart enough, I'm clever, I'm sad" are stories we tell about the character we are playing.

These stories make up our sense of self. But such limited descriptions can never capture the complexity and ever-evolving nature of the experience of being a human being. Moreover, such descriptions leave out the truth about ourselves: We are an expression of life, a manifestation of divine energy, an expression of love, eternal and unblemished. Whether you believe these things about yourself or not, they are true. Not believing them doesn't change the truth, but it does change your experience of life, especially if you believe, instead, that you are what your mind says you are.

Everything we think about ourselves was learned. We were taught to see ourselves a certain way by those we grew up around and by our culture, particularly through the ever-present TV. We also came to conclusions about ourselves because of our experiences, which then became part of our self-image. These conclusions were those of a child who knew little about life, who blamed himself or herself whenever an adult was angry or unhappy. These conclusions were erroneous and limiting, but when we were children, it couldn't be otherwise.

As adults, it's important to examine the conclusions that make up our self-image and how we feel about ourselves. *I* thoughts are problematic because most of us have defined ourselves in untrue and limiting ways and have taken on self-images that make us unhappy and distrustful of ourselves and life.

Notice what you think and say about yourself. Notice how what you think and say about yourself makes you feel. Notice what you don't say about yourself—what you leave out. These statements determine how you feel about yourself. Becoming more aware of our thoughts about ourselves and our self-images is such important psychological work, because we are responsible for how we feel about ourselves and how we feel in general. Only we can change how we feel about ourselves and the emotional climate we live in.

Until we've done this work and seen through the false self, trying to feel good about ourselves becomes a major focus of our energy. We strive to accomplish things and struggle to do them right, to be more perfect, and to be smarter or better than others. The false self becomes the focus of a self-improvement project, which never lets us rest, never allows us to feel good and to just be.

It's wonderful to develop ourselves and our talents, to learn, and to accomplish things. But when feelings of unworthiness are driving these accomplishments, enjoying our accomplishments and enjoying life along the way becomes difficult. There's always more to be accomplished, more self-improvement necessary before we feel we can rest and be okay. Feelings of unworthiness are at the root of the stressful and overly busy lives so many of us lead.

This is not just a personal issue but a societal disease. Our society is a reflection of the feeling that so many of us have of never having or being enough, which results in striving for more and better of everything, particularly material things.

The universal story is: "I'm not good enough. Life isn't good enough!" Built into everyone's story is an *I* that needs to strive to be good enough and to make life turn out right. When the *me* does succeed at something, that feeling of finally being good enough is all too soon replaced by the old drumbeat: "I'm still not good enough! Life still isn't good enough!"

Substituting such erroneous thoughts with truer, more positive ones can be useful. However, true freedom from unworthiness comes from really seeing that our dissatisfaction with ourselves and with life comes only from thoughts we acquired in the past—from our conditioning. There's no truth in or substance to thoughts of unworthiness or lack or to the other negative thoughts associated with *I*.

Everyone has these thoughts because everyone has a false self and a sense of being a *me*. We can't get rid of *I* thoughts, although the negative ones might lessen and *I* thoughts in general might quiet down from doing emotional healing work and various spiritual practices, such as meditation. We have to learn to live with these self-referencing thoughts. The way to do that is to recognize them as the conditioning we were given.

What is it that can recognize the programming? What is it that can see the *I* thoughts and stories for what they are—the false self and a false reality? What can recognize such thoughts for what they are is who we really are. We are not what our thoughts tell us we are, but what is capable of being aware of such thoughts and of everything else. We are what is conscious of thoughts, including *I* thoughts!

The illusion is that we are the *I* who is thinking about itself and its life. But who and where is the *I* that is thinking? Can you find it? When you look for it, there's nothing there! All the *I* is, is self-images and thoughts about yourself and how your life is going. Although we need to refer to ourselves as *I* to function in the world as the character we are playing, our *I* thoughts immerse us in a virtual reality that takes us away from real life and our true self.

You don't have to do a thing about these *I* thoughts but notice them, and then get on with what's in front of you: What are you experiencing right here and now? What are you experiencing in your body, internally and through your senses? Emotions and thoughts about yourself might be part of your present moment experience, but what else is here? What intuitions, subtle urges, and inspirations are here right now? Are gratitude, expansiveness, beauty, love, peace, and joy here too, even just a little?

Thoughts about the past don't serve, the future isn't real, and our ideas about and objections to the present only keep us from really being in this amazing life and tapping into the wisdom of the beautiful being that we are. You are wise, loving, and creative. See what happens when you let yourself move beyond thoughts about *I,* when you're just in your life fresh and new, as that which is looking out of your eyes and moving your body. We are all much more amazing than we *think.*

Stories

What comes after *I* in most of our thoughts is a story, unless it's a simple statement of fact such as, "I had eggs for breakfast." These stories create the story of *me:* how I was in the past, how I'm doing now, what I want in the future, and what that will be like. It's natural to tell stories. As long as we have a mind, there will probably be stories going through it.

However, believing these stories affects how we feel and what we do. Stories create a lens through which we see life. The truer our stories are, that is, the closer to reality they are, the less they distort life and the happier and more functional we will be. Unfortunately, many of our stories are not very true and interfere with our functioning, happiness, and relationships.

The mind is obsessed with its stories about how life is going for *me*. Have you noticed? It's always checking to see how things are going for *me* and adjusting its story about *my life* accordingly. When something "good" happens, the story is a good one; when something "bad" happens, the story turns bad. On some days the story of *me* is going great, while on others it takes a terrible turn! This telling of stories turns life into a rollercoaster and a melodrama: One minute we're up, and one minute we're down, depending on how our story is going or on what specifics in our story we're focused on.

When the moment is stripped of any story about how our life is going, life is pretty simple and uncomplicated. Things are arising in the moment: sensations, thoughts, sights, sounds, intuitions, inspirations, urges to act, desires, and feelings. Those are all part of life happening in any moment. We respond or not to these things, and that's part of life happening as well.

In many moments, a thought shows up about how things are going. Often it's a story about not having something, wanting something, or not wanting to do or experience something. Whether the story is a good one or a bad one, real life is still showing up the way it always does, as sensations, thoughts, sights, sounds, intuitions, inspirations, urges to act, desires, and feelings. And the same things still need to get done: shower, cook, eat, get the children ready for school, work, do laundry, shop for groceries, walk the dog, exercise, answer email, put the children to bed. That's real life. Stripped of our stories, life is pretty simple.

Most would agree that a good story is preferable to a bad one. Good stories make us feel good, while bad ones make us feel bad. Stories color our experience of real life: When our story is good, we don't mind taking a shower, doing laundry, going to the grocery store, and doing all the other things that are part of real life, part of the moment. We feel happier and behave more lovingly when our story about how our life is going is a good one. When our story is a bad one, whatever is showing up in life tends to feel like a burden and a problem, even things that might not ordinarily be. We resist life. We feel bad, and we're likely to behave badly toward others.

What we may not realize is that we have some choice about our stories. Although they show up unbidden by us, once we become aware of them, we don't have to buy into them. Once we realize that they are only the mind's stories and have little to do with real life, we can more easily disregard them. Or we can replace the stories that make us feel bad with ones that make us feel more at peace. This is called reframing, and it's one way we can use our intelligence to change our mental state and shift our consciousness. Seeing life as a problem, as the ego does, keeps us stuck in the ego's world. Reframing the stories that make us contract eliminates the sense of a problem and allows us to relax into Stillness. More will be said about reframing in the next chapter.

Our stories serve no purpose, really. What good is it to evaluate life? But that's just what the egoic mind does. It declares that something is good or bad. It has a black and white view of life, which denies and overlooks life's beauty and depth. When we stop identifying with these stories—when we stop assuming they're ours and they're true—then these stories stop influencing our experience of life and our behavior. And we stop being at the mercy of the ego's emotional rollercoaster.

Good stories, such as, "Everyone likes me, I'm so lucky, I have a great job, I have plenty of money, I look great!" are better than bad stories because good stories make it easier to relax and enjoy life just the way it is. The story itself doesn't make us happy, but a good story makes it easier to experience Stillness, which makes us happy. Good stories help us move out of bad stories and experience our true nature.

When we're caught in a bad or sad story, we become focused on trying to fix the problem described by the story and the negative feelings generated by the story, without realizing that the mind created that story—and that problem. The mind made the story and the problem up! A problem is a concept. There's no such thing as a problem, only the egoic mind defining something as a problem. The mind defines events as problems. In this way, it gives life a negative spin, while life is just doing what life does.

Our minds love to tell stories! But that doesn't make our stories real, true, or worthy of our attention. No story is ever true. Life is much too complex, ever-changing, and mysterious to be captured by any story that our mind might tell. If our stories helped us function better, I'd say, "Keep them!" But they don't. Instead, they do the opposite. Most of all, they stress us out and make us unhappy. When we aren't involved in the *me* and the stories it's spinning, or when we don't give those tales our attention, we experience life just as it is, and life is always good. Being aware of and disengaging from our stories is the antidote to the pain and stress caused by them.

Another antidote to a negative story, besides telling a good story, is to tell a true story. A true story is one that's true all the time. A story that is not very true isn't true all the time. An example of a true story is: "Sometimes it rains." An example of a story that isn't very true is: "It always rains on my day off."

You can tell the difference between a true story and one that isn't very true by how it makes you feel. A true story results in relaxation or a neutral response, while a story that isn't very true results in unpleasant feelings and tension. Negative feelings and tension are signs that the mind is telling a story that isn't very true.

The ego's stories, when they are believed, create agitation emotionally, mentally, and even physically. What often follows a story is an embellishment of it or a defense of it—evidence to support it, which creates further emotional agitation. If that story is shared with others, it causes agitation in them, and they tend to respond with stories of their own, causing more agitation. The ego loves this agitation. It loves to stir up emotions. When your emotions or other people's have been triggered, you can be sure that the ego is behind that. No one needs such stories.

True stories have the opposite effect: They calm us and bring us into Stillness. When you tell true stories, such as "Love is more important than appearances" or "All is well," your body and entire being relax. Then peace, love and wisdom can flow. From Stillness, either true stories are spoken or nothing at all. This is a very different state from the egoic state of consciousness.

The stories that come from Stillness celebrate love, growth, beauty, goodness, and the miraculousness of life. They express kindness, acceptance, and gratitude for life. They make us feel that all is well and that we are loved and cared for by some greater Intelligence, which is the truth. They open the heart and cause other people's hearts to open.

Judgments

No good comes from judging. Judgments cause stress to ourselves and others. They undermine our relationships and our happiness. What a burden it is to be a judge! After all, how happy are you when you're feeling judgmental? It's no better to be judged. Whether we're judging or being judged, we feel contracted, tense, and small. No matter what side of a judgment you're on, judgments don't feel good.

If peace, love, and happiness are important to you, then eliminating judging is a way to bring those good feeling into your life and your loved one's lives. Although we can't keep judgments from arising in our mind, we can change our relationship to them: We can become aware of a judgmental thought, withdraw our agreement from it, and choose to not give voice to it. We can stop jumping on the judgment bandwagon.

Not judging isn't as difficult as you might think. It's actually a big relief to not feel that you have to have an opinion or know what's right for someone else. The key to not judging is seeing the truth about your judgments. The biggest truth is that judging others kills love, sometimes quickly and sometimes slowly. Judgments don't serve anyone, although we tend to think that they demonstrate how smart and discriminating we are. In truth, judgments come from the ego and serve only the ego, whose goal is to be superior and right.

You can become free from the stress caused by your judgments by seeing that they are not yours. What I mean by this is that judging is an automatic response to others and to life on the part of our ego. It isn't a function of our true nature or necessary for our survival. Judgments don't come from a place of wisdom and discrimination, which are qualities of our true nature.

True wisdom is experienced as a knowing, an insight, an intuition, or a big yes, not as judgmental thoughts or opinions about ourselves or others. The ego is a cruel and petty inner tyrant. If we let it, it will make us and everyone around us unhappy. When we are involved with it mentally or giving voice to it, we feel contracted and tense, which is the opposite of how we feel when we're in touch with our true nature and sharing with others from there.

Since this voice in our head isn't our true voice but reflects the ego and our conditioning, and since this voice isn't wise and doesn't bring love and happiness, it can be ignored. When we do that, life goes much better. Ignoring our judgments isn't repressing our feelings but avoiding creating unnecessary negative feelings, which judgments cause. If we can do this, we'll be available to experience our true self's response to the moment instead of the ego's. There's something guiding us that is much wiser than the ego, which naturally expresses kindness toward others, if we're willing to give our attention to it instead of the ego.

We seem to have two sides to ourselves—the good or nice *me* and the bad or mean *me.* The good news is that the unkind *me* is not you at all. The loving you is the real you. The true self responds to life with acceptance, love, compassion, and wisdom. In any moment, we can choose to express our true nature instead of the ego. What makes this difficult is that the voice in our head often has our attention. Consequently, we don't notice the beauty and love that are ever-present within us and in the world around us. So we respond to the voice in our head instead of the beauty.

We tend to feel that our judgments are true and valuable, but that's an illusion. Instead, judgments are some of the most stressful thoughts we have. Judgments are no way to try to improve yourself, as you've undoubtedly discovered. And they're no way to improve others. Judgments have never changed anyone, at least not without harming the relationship. All they do is alienate others and invite retaliation.

Judgments are very often an attempt to change others or get our way by assuming a superior position. For example, you might say, "If you weren't so scatterbrained, maybe you could be on time." The ego tries to manipulate others by putting them down. This is not a winning strategy. It only makes people withdraw their love or not want to comply.

When you're on the receiving end of a judgment, the best advice is to try not to attack the person who is judging you. Recognize that he or she is caught in judgment, have compassion for the unpleasantness of that state (because we all know it), and try to respond in a way that will diffuse that person's ego. If you respond with compassion, that person may be able to put aside the judgment and be more understanding. Acknowledge how the one who's judging you is feeling: "I can see this is really important to you" or "I get where you're coming from." Then apologize if that's appropriate. You might explain how you see things and where you're coming from, based on your own conditioning.

The way to not take judgments and unkindness personally is to realize that how others behave toward you isn't personal. How they behave isn't about you as much as it is about their ideas about you and their ideas in general. They're reacting for the most part to how they imagine you to be and to how they think you or your relationship should be.

For example, if your wife tells you that you're uncaring for forgetting to pick up something from the store, she's upset because her expectation wasn't met and because she concluded that you didn't care about her. She took your mistake personally, and now it's up to you to try to not take her judgment personally.

If she felt disregarded as a child, then whenever something happens that makes her feel disregarded, the old feelings of unworthiness and shame will be triggered. When such feelings are reignited, we tend to blame or attack our partner. Aren't relationships great!

For relationships to flourish, it is so important to be aware of and investigate our beliefs, judgments, opinions, desires, and other conditioning and to hold them lightly. They are only ideas, after all. They aren't more important than love and connection. But if we make them more important, our relationships will be full of struggle and stress, and love might not survive.

Once we learn to hold our own thoughts, opinions, judgments, desires, and beliefs more lightly, it's easier to hold other people's more lightly. In other words, when we're less identified with our own ego, it's much easier to be detached from other people's egos. Instead of reacting to a judgment or unkindness as we might have in the past, we recognize that it's coming from that person's ego and respond compassionately. Such a response will often elicit the other person's compassion. Just as judgments invite the ego into a relationship, love and compassion invite the true self.

The antidote to judgment is accepting people the way they are and not imposing our desires and expectations on them. Our desires and how we'd like someone to behave are not more important than love. If we make them more important than love, we will lose love. Our desires and expectations are part of our conditioning. When we try to impose our conditioning on others, we lose love. But when we accept others as they are, love flows. And that can only be good for everyone.

We have the power to not let judgments interfere with love by not giving voice to them. Notice a judgment as it shows up in your mind and then put your attention on what you love about that person or on anything else but your judgment. We have the power to choose peace, love, and relationship over our judgments once we see how damaging, counterproductive, and useless our judgments are.

When we judge ourselves or others, we are assuming that we or someone else could be different. However, many factors contribute to how we respond and behave in any moment, such as personality, maturity, soul age, genetic inheritance, past experiences, desires, beliefs, self-images, and other perceptions and conditioning. In many respects, all of this conditioning predetermines or at least makes it likely that we will respond a certain way in any given moment. Until these patterns, beliefs, and other conditioning are seen for what they are, they're likely to shape our behavior unconsciously. To expect people to be any different than they are is to not appreciate that they're doing the best they can, given their history, personality, body-mind, and conditioning. When you catch yourself judging someone, it helps to remember this.

When we examine our own past and behavior, we can have the same compassion: Could I really have responded any differently than I did at the time? Not really. Many factors lead up to every response we have to life. Until we become conscious of these factors and make an effort to respond differently, we're likely to continue to act out our conditioning. The freedom to choose other than the conditioned response is only possible after we've seen the conditioned self for what it is. Even then, not identifying with the conditioned self can be very challenging.

When we're not identified with the judging, conditioned self but in touch with our true nature, life feels lighter and is experienced as a gift *just as it is*. It is so much work to try to get the imperfect character that we are to be more perfect and to get other imperfect characters to be more perfect according to our ideas of perfection. We can never succeed. The good news is that we don't have to. We can just let ourselves and everyone else be the way they are. What a relief!

Once we recognize who we are, we accept the imperfections (which are actually perfect!) of this character and those of others. The character can be whatever it is, while we bask in the perfection of our being and of all of life. All is well, even these characters and everything they have ever done. Mistakes and learning from our mistakes is part of the natural unfolding of life, as we evolve toward being kinder and wiser human beings.

Self-Criticism

Many of us have a strong inner critic, and we take its criticism to heart. No doubt this is because its source is our childhood and the criticism we received then. When we were a child, we assumed that our parents' perceptions were the truth, so when they criticized us, we believed them: "You're so careless! Why don't you listen? Your head is in the clouds. You'd better start paying attention or you'll never make it in life."

Surely when our parents said such things, they thought they were being helpful. But although their intentions may have been good, the result wasn't. Now we carry around with us our parents' words and how they made us feel. Whenever we make a mistake, the same shame and feelings of inadequacy come up as when we were young.

Mistakes are normal, kids are imperfect, adults are imperfect. But as children, we're likely to have concluded that making mistakes meant we were bad or stupid or that we wouldn't do well in life or any number of other things. It's no wonder many of us are paralyzed by new situations and challenges, because we're afraid we'll make a mistake. We may stop ourselves from going after what we want, trying or learning new things, developing our talents, growing, and having fun, all because we're afraid of feeling those familiar feelings of failure from long ago. Parental criticism becomes self-criticism. We learned to do that perfectly!

Criticism feels terrible, whether it's from others or we're doing it to ourselves. Just as our parents probably thought they were helping us by criticizing us, we may think we're doing ourselves a favor by doing the same. We may believe this inner critic is watching our back or making us a better person, but the opposite is true. When we are self-critical, we're more stressed and less relaxed, more apt to make mistakes, less confident, less attractive to others, less loving and generous, and less in touch with our inner wisdom.

The good news is that self-criticism isn't actually you criticizing you, but your egoic mind criticizing you. The real you has nothing but love, acceptance, and compassion for the character that you are. Within our dual nature, we have the capacity to criticize and hate ourselves as well as the capacity to love ourselves. Once we realize that all criticism comes from the ego and doesn't serve us, we can begin to free ourselves from this limiting voice and, more importantly, begin to hear our true voice of compassion, love, and wisdom.

It's often said that we can't really love others until we first love ourselves, and this is so true. We all want love and we all want to love others. What makes being loving difficult is this voice of criticism. If it weren't there, loving ourselves and others would be easy!

Fortunately, the voice of self-criticism doesn't have to go away to become free of it. You know that old saying, "Sticks and stones will break my bones, but names will never hurt me"? This is true of the egoic mind, which calls us names, shames us, and makes us feel guilty and inadequate. The mind's words don't have to hurt us. They are just words, just thoughts. We don't have to empower them with our belief, once we see that they are lies.

It's not necessarily easy to disengage from the inner voice of criticism, especially if we've believed it for a long time. But with greater awareness of our thoughts, we can wake up from the illusion that our egoic mind is a true and meaningful voice. We wake up to the truth that we don't need the voice in our head, we have never needed it, and it has only caused a lot of suffering. As difficult as it may be to change this habit of believing the mind, living with this voice is much more difficult.

What is it that can stand up to this voice and say, "Thanks, but no thanks"? That's the real you! It's right here, right now, accessible in any moment whenever you call forth your own inner strength and wisdom. Who you really are isn't an abstraction—something out there in the ethers—but what is living your life. The more you turn away from the egoic mind and access your loving, wise, strong, accepting, and compassionate self, the more available this self becomes. Whenever you turn away from self-criticism, the connection to your true self is strengthened. The more you do this, the easier it becomes, until one day you realize that the voice of self-criticism is a mere whisper or completely gone.

This is how the egoic mind and the negative feelings it produces are quelled: We stop believing the voice in our head and, consequently, stop producing negative emotions. Instead of criticism, we bring compassion to our humanness, failings, and mistakes. If we do find ourselves stuck in negativity or acting it out, we notice that and then bring compassion to ourselves for this very normal, human occurrence. It's okay to not be perfect. How do I know? Because no one is or ever has been.

We are all in the same boat—all flawed, all struggling, all wanting to be happy and sometimes failing miserably at it. When you can love yourself just the way you are and have compassion for yourself, then it becomes easy to love and have compassion for others. Be kind to yourself!

Self-Doubt

Self-doubt, like so many other thoughts produced by the ego, arises automatically and regularly, whether warranted or not. We are programmed to doubt ourselves. Whenever an opportunity arises, self-doubt shows up. Those of us who had harsh parents experience more than the usual dose of self-doubt. And the more we've believed this voice of doubt, the more it's been strengthened and the more credible it seems. Since self-doubt is part of the human condition, we might as well expect it and welcome it when it shows up and say, "Thanks for sharing," and then get on with whatever we were doing.

The point is that self-doubt is not the voice of wisdom, working in our behalf to make us a better person, but an automatic, programmed response that arises whenever we're faced with a decision or trying to accomplish something. This voice has nothing for us and only undermines our confidence and clarity. Self-doubt is what most stands in the way of following our intuition, which is the true voice of wisdom.

It's easy enough to tell the difference between self-doubt and our inner wisdom because they feel very different. Self-doubt makes us feel bad. If we listen to it, we feel stressed-out, contracted, confused, and even afraid, which are all signs of the ego. On the other hand, when we're in touch with our inner wisdom, we feel relaxed, at ease, strong, and clear.

Our inner wisdom doesn't stir up our emotions or use scary thoughts to guide us, like the ego does. In fact, our inner wisdom rarely uses thoughts at all. It speaks to us intuitively and feels the same way that advice from a trusted mentor might. Rather than making us feel bad or discouraged, we feel grateful for these intuitions: "Ah, yes. I need to be aware of that."

The antidote to self-doubt is quite simple. If it's a doubting thought, don't believe it. Let your intuition guide you instead: Does moving forward or the thought of moving forward with something feel like a yes in your body, which is experienced as expansion, relaxation, peace, and joy? Or does it feel like a no in your body, which is experienced as contraction and tension? Our bodies register truth — the heart's truth. If something is true to our heart, it feels good and right; if not, it feels bad and not right. The egoic mind causes confusion by arguing with these intuitive messages from the heart: "But what about...? But what if.... But I can't...."

Self-doubt isn't useful. We don't need it and it isn't helpful. It's a lie. Once you really get this, you can disengage from the mind's doubts and move forward. Awareness of a lie frees us from it.

Thoughts Related to Dissatisfaction

Much of the dissatisfaction we experience is produced by the ego and has no value or purpose other than to drive life forward in the way the ego sees fit. The ego is in the business of creating dissatisfaction, so no matter how ideal our situation may be, the ego will find something to be dissatisfied with. As a result, we can't necessarily trust feelings of dissatisfaction and restlessness. They'll always be there to one extent or another. All this dissatisfaction and restlessness make the world go around, in that these feelings create a lot of inner and outer busy-ness. But to what effect?

This dissatisfaction spawns any number of stressful and unnecessary thoughts, including complaints, fantasies, desires, and the fear that we'll continue to be dissatisfied. Instead of just noticing the dissatisfaction, accepting it, and allowing it to be there for however long it lasts (all feelings come and go in their own time), we are likely to do any number of things to try to get rid of it.

The egoic mind spends countless hours dreaming about what it would be like if things were better and devising plans and strategies to change whatever we're dissatisfied with, whether it's our health, our housing situation, our job, our friendships, our partner, or our children (or lack thereof). To try to get what it wants, the egoic mind involves us in a lot of doing: trying to change something, working harder to make money to change it, and complaining and talking to friends about our "problem."

To cope with the dissatisfaction that it creates, the ego often drives us to overindulge in food, alcohol, drugs, shopping, or other addictive behaviors. Workaholism is often driven by this same dissatisfaction, as one puts off being happy right now for an imagined happier future that is assumed to be without dissatisfaction.

All of these activities, which take a lot of our time, are intended to do away with, mask, or distract us from our dissatisfaction. There's nothing wrong with trying to change what we don't like or going after what we do like, but allowing our dissatisfaction to shape our life creates a different experience than pursuing things for reasons other than dissatisfaction. There's another way to live.

We might think that if we weren't dissatisfied, we would do nothing; we'd just sit and stare at a wall. But that's not true. We would still work, we would still play, and we would still be social. We would still do many of the things that our dissatisfaction motivates us to do, but we would do them for a different reason, not to cure our dissatisfaction. We would do them for the joy of doing them. We would do them because doing them came out of the flow. We don't need dissatisfaction to move our life forward. Something else is moving our life forward and using joy and love to do that, not the stress that comes from feeling that our life or we aren't good enough.

The way out of dissatisfaction is just letting dissatisfaction be there. What if you were okay with feeling dissatisfied? What if you just let dissatisfaction be there? Dissatisfaction doesn't have to be a problem. Expect to be dissatisfied, because the ego generates dissatisfaction constantly. Dissatisfaction comes and then goes when we turn our attention to life and get lost in the moment.

You can make friends with dissatisfaction. Just let it be and recognize it for what it is: the ongoing state of the ego. Then find the place within you that isn't dissatisfied, the place where all is well. It's always possible to find within us that which is satisfied with life, but we have to be willing to take our focus off the dissatisfaction and look for what is already and always satisfied.

Our true self is an experience of satisfaction and contentment with life, no matter what is happening. In any moment, there are two possible experiences: the experience of dissatisfaction that the ego is having or the experience of satisfaction that our being is having. Once you recognize these two very different states within yourself, you have some choice about what you will experience. You can choose to identify with the ego and its experience of dissatisfaction or with the experience of peace and contentment.

Anytime you feel dissatisfied, you can remember that this is your ego's state, not your true state. Then you can search for what is a truer state, a state of peace and contentment. If you look for it, you can find it. It's just that we often don't look for or notice the subtle peace and contentment that are always here, because the mind keeps our attention focused on its complaints, fantasies, desires, fears, strategies, and plans.

It's so easy to be dissatisfied. It's the easiest thing in the world, because it's easy to find fault. What is this aspect of the mind that finds fault with things? Is it intelligent? Is it wise? Is it even necessary to find fault with things?

Finding fault is what the ego does and what it's programmed to do, which is why finding fault is so easy. We are all programmed to find fault, to judge, to criticize, and to tell stories about our experience. But how valuable is this? Finding fault is not the same thing as discrimination, although fault-finding and judgment masquerade as discrimination. Finding fault has no value at all. We can live much more happily if we don't give our attention to such thoughts.

Experiencing life purely, without the ego's judgments, complaints, likes, and dislikes is much more difficult. Although it's natural, the natural state isn't as easy to experience as the egoic state of consciousness. To live from your natural state requires seeing dissatisfaction for what it is and realizing that you don't need to get rid of or fix it. There's another possibility, which is to notice the dissatisfaction, let it be there, and then return to your natural state of contentment.

The truth is that there is something to be satisfied with in every moment. Our true self is satisfied even with what the ego is dissatisfied with. In even the most challenging moments, it's possible to find something to be satisfied with. Happiness is largely a matter of focusing on what *is* here, what is beautiful, what is lovable, and what there is to be grateful for in this moment rather than on what isn't here or what we aren't satisfied with.

However, being in touch with our true self doesn't mean we won't ever change something we don't like. If change or action is called for, we'll be moved to act appropriately, because Stillness is a place of clarity from which right action arises. On the other hand, discontentment, because it's created by the ego, is a place of confusion, lack of clarity, and missteps.

Trying to fix our dissatisfaction takes a lot of energy. Meanwhile, something more meaningful and fulfilling than those activities might be coming out of the flow to do. If not, then not giving your attention to dissatisfaction will allow whatever you're doing to be more enjoyable. Doing still happens when we're content with what is, and what we do will be aligned with our true self. That can only bring true happiness and further contentment.

What to Do

One of the questions that commonly keeps us absorbed in our thoughts is the question of what to do: "Should I stay in my relationship or not? Should I quit my job or not? Should I get a master's degree or not? Should I relocate or not?" Many feel moved to make a change, but they don't know if they can trust that or what to do about it, so they're left feeling confused and stuck.

Such questions, themselves, don't necessarily cause stress, but the confusion and mental spinning of wheels that tends to accompany them can be stressful and draining. Confusion and difficulty trusting ourselves are caused by the egoic mind and aren't necessary to the choice-making process. If you are feeling confused about a decision, that's a sign that the ego is involved in the choice-making process.

Confusion about what to do is often symptomatic of having "one foot in and one foot out" regarding an issue: We may want to leave a relationship, but we don't want to hurt someone; we may want to leave a job or move, but we're afraid to; or we may want to go to school, but we see too many hurdles. So we have one foot in our current situation and another that wants to walk away from it. The same kind of confusion can happen around more everyday choices. For example, you sign up for a retreat, and then the mind second-guesses that choice, and you're left feeling stuck and confused.

Not being able to commit to one side or the other in a relationship or some other issue is uncomfortable and stressful. More importantly, whether it's a job, a place, or a relationship, if we are halfway in and halfway out, we're probably not involved and invested enough in that situation for it to be enjoyable and meaningful. Wanting life to be different makes us not want to be present and spoils the enjoyment that's possible within that situation.

When we feel moved to do something that isn't easy for us to do, such as leave a relationship or change careers, the heart is usually urging this. Saying no to the heart is difficult because its urges are compelling, and yet circumstances might make it difficult to say yes to it: Changes have to be made, sometimes very difficult ones. That's where the ego is likely to come in with stoppers: "But what about...."

When our heart chooses something, it's for a reason, although these reasons are likely to be a mystery to us and may not seem reasonable at all! Our heart's choices don't always seem sensible and practical even though they're right for us at the time. This can make following the heart especially challenging.

The heart doesn't give us reasons for why we feel the way we feel. But when we feel the yes of the heart, we don't need reasons. We just feel a yes about doing something, and that's reason enough—until we start to question that decision, or others question it.

Here's the rub: The ego *does* need reasons. It makes choices by examining reasons for and against a possible choice. So what often happens is that our ego or other people's egos come in with objections that muddy the clarity that we had about a choice that came from our heart.

The ego's reasons are reasonable: "It's expensive, I have to take off of work, and I have to fly across the country." The funny thing is, our life isn't really very well guided or lived by making such reasons primary. The heart does know the way and will take us where we need and truly want to go, and the outcome is often quite unpredictable from our current standpoint. If we make the ego's practicalities or shoulds primary in our decisions, we may lose our way and miss out on certain possibilities. Being mindful of the practicalities surrounding our choices makes sense, but we often give too much weight to practicalities. Some of the most important choices in our life are not very practical or are riddled with hurdles.

I'll give you an example from my own life. When I was thirty-two, I realized that I didn't want to teach children anymore and that I wanted to become a counselor or therapist. At the time, I owned a small preschool. How could I change careers? How could I get a master's degree? I lived in rural Wisconsin, an hour and a half from a university, I was divorced, and I had a four year-old son. Shortly after asking myself this question, I was at a party, and an acquaintance was talking about going back to school. I knew she had even fewer financial resources than I had.

I asked her how she was going to do that. She said she was getting a loan.

This may seem like an obvious solution, but it was a revelation to me at the time. So that became my plan. I would sell my preschool business, move, get a loan, and go back to school. I was fortunate to have a buyer for my business. With two-thousand dollars to my name from that, I was ready to go.

Then two days before my move, my car's engine died about a quarter of a mile from my house after doing some grocery shopping. This was fairly accommodating of my car, since I lived eleven miles from town. Another hurdle, though! Or so it seemed. But as it turned out, I didn't need a car where I was going, and in fact a car would have been more of a problem than an advantage in that college town. Life provides what we need in order to follow our heart. It even takes away what we don't need.

When we follow our heart, that doesn't mean we won't experience difficulties or hurdles, because any choice is bound to have challenges. But when we're following our heart, we find the resources to handle the hurdles or we're just willing to do whatever it takes to overcome them.

Sometimes we let our mind talk us out of following our heart at the thought of or in the face of certain hurdles. At any point along the way, the ego can interrupt our momentum and stop us short, and we're left feeling confused and stuck or depressed. When that happens, it's unfortunate, as it is always easier and more rewarding to follow our heart, no matter what the ego says about the possible difficulties.

One reason following our heart is difficult is that shooting down a particular choice is extremely easy. Finding reasons to *not* do something is simple. The ego has a very easy job. The ego even second-guesses its own decisions. You can't win with the ego. If the ego is involved, no matter what you choose, you're left feeling stuck and confused.

When the ego isn't playing the role of the stopper, it takes on the role of the pusher. When we've finally gotten unstuck and are in the midst of making a change, the ego often pushes us to make decisions before clarity naturally arises within that process of change. The ego wants clarity *now,* but clarity about how to proceed happens in its own time. Sometimes we have to patiently wait for life to show us the next step. Sometimes not having clarity is the clarity.

Clarity comes from the deep wellspring of our being. It comes from life as it unfolds, and when it arises isn't under our command. Life unfolds in its own time, and although our will is part of that unfolding, our will by no means determines all the events that allow our life to move forward in the direction of our heart's choice. So when we're making a change, we need to continually listen to the heart and not to the ego's push and impatience. Living this way takes trust, and our ego does not trust life.

Solving Problems

The egoic mind makes it its business to solve our problems. Of course, many of our problems are things that the mind defined as a problem in the first place, because of dissatisfaction. We have real problems, and we have things that the mind makes into problems. The mind often turns the way things are into a problem or turns things we can't do anything about into a problem. For example, not being in a relationship might feel like a problem. But is that really a problem? Only if you *think* it is. And just because others might agree that something is a problem doesn't mean it is. Egoic minds think alike.

A real problem is something that needs to be handled, something that requires your attention, like a chipped tooth, getting your car fixed, or needing to find a job. Even these things don't have to feel like a problem. The mind makes so many things feel like a problem, when they're just part of life.

We do have problems that need solving, and for this we've been given an intellect, which we use to think, plan, and reason with. This rational aspect of the mind is distinct from the egoic mind, which could be termed irrational. We need our intellect, but we don't need the egoic mind. Using our intellect to solve problems is not stressful. It isn't stressful to get information or talk with someone about an issue, fill out a job application, or do whatever you might need to do to solve a problem, unless you make it stressful by what you tell yourself while you're doing these things.

Stress comes into the picture when we turn the things we need to do or turn the way life is into a problem, tell ourselves it shouldn't be happening, complain, feel victimized or angry, worry, or wish we were having some other experience. Worrying, complaining, wishing, obsessing about the problem, or getting angry doesn't help us solve the problem. These activities only get us more deeply entrenched in the egoic mind and its negativity, discouragement, and limited view of solutions.

The egoic mind chews on a problem like a dog with a bone, refusing to relax or let go of it until exhaustion sets in. The mind pushes for solutions before it's time for a solution to be known. Solutions show up when they show up, on their own schedule, not ours. But the ego must have a plan and the solution now!

We wear ourselves out thinking about our problems and planning for every possible contingency: "What will I do if I don't get that job, and what will I do if I do, and what if I don't want that job, and what if I don't do well at it, and what will everyone think if I get that job, and what will everyone think if I don't, and...?" The fear that the egoic mind brings to planning and solving problems makes these activities so stressful. The egoic mind makes life so difficult—so stressful. It works so hard trying to figure out things that can't be figured out or don't even need to be figured out.

Life doesn't have to be so stressful. If we can learn to use our intellect when it's needed and put it down when it's not needed and not let the egoic mind chew on the problem in between, we'll experience very little stress.

Life has a way of bringing us solutions to our problems. We may have to do some footwork and study, talk to some people, and take action in other ways, all of which take time. Finding a solution to a problem is a process that unfolds over time, as we feel our way through this process and as answers about what to do arise in their own time, out of the flow. The impatience and tension created by the egoic mind make it difficult to contact the natural flow of life, which is bringing us what we need to solve our real problems, the ones that have come out of the flow to be solved.

Once you really see that trying to figure things out when they can't be known, trying to plan every detail ahead of time, worrying, and complaining don't serve you or the problem-solving process, then not feeding the egoic mind becomes easier. If we feed our thoughts with more thoughts, the egoic mind just gets stronger. Although we can't keep such thoughts from popping into our mind, we can learn to turn away from them instead of hopping on the train of thoughts and riding it. Notice how you don't need to plan, figure out, and strategize to the extent that your mind suggests. Do what needs to be done to solve something and then let the mind rest. In the resting, come real solutions to real problems.

Shoulds

Shoulds are statements with "should" in them. Shoulds are tricky because many of the shoulds in our mind contain very good advice, while others are not so useful or even true. It's helpful to know that you should brush your teeth twice a day, that you should be kind to others, and that you should look both ways before crossing the street. These are useful guidelines. We were taught certain things, and these become rules to live by: shoulds. The problem is that not everything we were taught is true or always true or a good rule for us personally to live by in the moment in which the should arises.

We were taught things like: "You should obey your parents. You shouldn't get angry. You should go to church. You shouldn't talk to strangers. You should go to college. You shouldn't cry. You should always tell the truth." While these might have been useful instructions when we were growing up or at other points along the way, are they useful to you now, in this moment?

Shoulds are only a problem if we blindly and rigidly follow them without examining them for how true they are for us right now. Although as adults, we now have the ability to do this examination, we still often act as children in the face of a should, assuming it's always true and the sky will fall down if we don't adhere to it.

Even though we acquired many of our beliefs as children, as adults, we need to take responsibility for what we believe and how we behave based on those beliefs, because what we believe will determine how happy we are. Given this, it's important to examine our conditioning, including the shoulds. Some of our shoulds don't make us better people, but only take us away from what might make us happy and fulfilled.

For example, my father was a doctor, an ophthalmologist. However, he didn't want to be a doctor, but he was afraid to disappoint his father and mother. He worked very hard his entire life, but he wasn't a happy man. He coped by eating and drinking too much. Nearly every evening he would burst into anger. He had a stroke in his fifties, a pacemaker in his sixties, and died of cancer in his seventies. Sadly, he died with many regrets. Following shoulds can rob us of our health and our soul.

The egoic mind is very quick to tell us what to do and not do—and so are other people's egoic minds. One of the ego's personas is the parent or authority figure. If we aren't conscious of this parental voice, we may find ourselves obeying it without questioning it, just as we did when we were young.

However, since the buck stops with you, it's best not to give your power away to your egoic mind or other people's without first checking in with your heart. The heart is where the truth lies for *you* about how to move through life. It is your life to live, not anyone else's. Living someone else's life, as my father did, is very hard to do. It's very stressful and not very happy.

Can anyone else know what's right for you as reliably as you can? Inside, you have the most dependable compass for knowing how to move in the world, more dependable than other people or your own conditioning. The guidance system we've each been given tells us what's true *now* for us, not at some other point in time or for some other person. It's specially designed for us. So if a should is in alignment with what your heart says, then you *should* do it! If it isn't, then you shouldn't.

This guidance system doesn't speak to us in shoulds but through more subtle signals and intuitions. These register in our body, especially in the area of the heart, and a knowing arises as an "aha" in our mind. This intuitive process happens in a split second, so if we're lost in thought, we might miss it. These communications from our heart feel good, even euphoric. How gracious of Life to point the way with good feelings! And the unpleasant feelings and depression we experience when we believe the mind's lies and half-truths are how Life shows us which directions *not* to go in. How benevolent of Life.

The funny thing is that when we're tuned in to the deeper guidance system of the heart, we don't need even the seemingly useful shoulds that our mind or other people's produce because we'll naturally act appropriately and safely. We are all wise at our core. We've already integrated all the conditioning we need to keep us safe—it's already in our bones. We don't really need the voice in our head to remind us of what we already know. Do you still need it to tell you to look both ways before crossing a street or to not touch a hot stove? When we're fully present in the moment, we are tuned in to this guidance system and naturally respond to it. Life unfolds simply and easily, uncomplicated by the confusion, fears, and guilt of the mind.

I understand that not listening to the voice in your head and trusting this inner guidance instead might sound airy-fairy to some, because that's how the egoic mind does see what I am suggesting. And yet, everyone knows what it feels like to be tuned in to the heart and in the flow of life. Once you shift your trust from the egoic mind to the heart, you begin to live more from that place of Stillness, out of which all of life comes. This is a place of wisdom, a place you can trust.

An antidote to the contraction and stress caused by certain shoulds that show up in our mind is to turn them into coulds: "I *should* go to the wedding" becomes "I *could* go to the wedding." This little trick allows more possibilities to be included. Shoulds narrow our choices down to one, which isn't exactly a choice and which may not be the right choice for you, even if other people think it is. Coulds open up our options: "I could go to the wedding or I could stay home and learn a new piece on the piano or I could have a day by myself to sit by the lake or...."

When more possibilities are included, it becomes easier to recognize what your heart really wants to do. Which option feels like a big yes? You may discover that you really do want to go to the wedding. It's much more pleasant to go to a wedding knowing that you want to go there than out of obligation.

I used to feel that my husband should be as neat and clean as I was. And I used to feel that the house should be kept neat and clean at all times. "It's just *right* to be neat and clean," I thought. "It's a sign of good character, a sign of a good woman." Because I saw things this way, there was tension in our relationship around this. As insignificant as this issue may seem, it was the biggest issue in our relationship when we first got together—big to me at least. It seemed so inconsiderate of him to not be willing to change for me. He should be more like me! Now, there's a stressful thought! What a lie that is.

It took me a while to realize that the problem wasn't him. He was perfectly content with a messy, dirty house! Nothing in him told him that things should be different. The problem was within me, with my demand—my conditioning—that he should be like me.

Once I clearly saw that it was my conditioning that made me think that the house should look a certain way and that how it looked implied something about me as a woman, I stopped expecting my husband to be different. If I wanted the house to be neat and clean, then it was up to me to make it that way. If I was going to march to that conditioning, which was my choice, why make him march to it too? The funny thing is that when I stopped being angry at my husband and expecting him to be more like me, he actually became more like me—willingly of his own accord. When we are happy and giving, our partner is naturally happy and giving.

I'm grateful that my husband is different from me in this way because these differences forced me to grow. They helped me realize that my conditioning to be neat is no more right than his conditioning to not be neat and that my conditioning might not even be right for me. This realization inspired me to experiment with how I did things and to learn to clean the house with more joy.

It didn't feel good to be at the mercy of my shoulds. I felt like a scowling scullery maid whenever I cleaned. It wasn't pretty. Now, if I choose to be neat and clean, I realize it's a choice and not a should. I *could* clean the house — if that's what's coming out of the flow, meaning if I can do it with joy.

So another problem with shoulds is that they can take the fun out of life. Even when we like doing something (I actually like to clean), if we feel we *should* do it, that creates inner resistance, just as the shoulds that came from our parents did and the shoulds that come from others often do. When we are in resistance, it becomes difficult to know what we want to do, what our heart wants, where our joy lies. Shoulds weren't a particularly effective way to motivate us as children, and they aren't now either. Following shoulds takes the juice out of life. If you're following a should and it's taking the joy out of life, then that's a should you shouldn't follow, at least not now.

Not following shoulds doesn't mean you'll behave badly or that you won't follow shoulds when appropriate. Not following my shoulds around housecleaning didn't mean I stopped cleaning the house; it just meant I did it with more awareness, choice, flexibility, and enjoyment. Our natural self knows how to behave and take care of ourselves.

We can trust our heart to lead us to activities that are wholesome, fulfilling, and supportive of our well-being. It's guilt, shame, and other negative emotions that lead to unwholesome things, such as addictions. Guilt and shame don't protect us from ourselves but only uphold the false self. If we aren't attending to the egoic mind, we won't get lost in negative feelings and we won't behave badly or unsafely. More importantly, we won't lose our way. Find out how to live *now* by turning your shoulds into coulds and opening up to all the options your heart comes up with.

Shoulds cause stress when we believe that we, other people, or things should be different than they are. Although there are plenty of times we would like things to be different, to think that something should be different than it is, is a place of contraction, a place of arguing with life. What use is that? Just notice how your body feels the next time you think something should be different. Notice the tension in your body. And notice how other people appear when they're caught in such thoughts. It's not a happy place.

Things can't be different than they are because they already are the way they are. To think that they could or should be different is to suffer, and why would you do that to yourself? Coulds and shoulds are the ego's point of view, of course. Believing things such as, "He shouldn't have done that! She shouldn't have died, That shouldn't have happened, I should have known better, Life shouldn't be so hard" is how we make life harder than it needs to be. To believe these thoughts feels bad. Why? Because they aren't true. They're more lies from the egoic mind.

Whenever we believe something that isn't true, we contract. This contraction tells us that we've bought into another one of the ego's lies. Can you think of a single exception to this? Contraction equals the ego.

Can your life be different than it is right now? Can events that already happened be different than they were? We have to learn to accept life as it is, or we will suffer. So much of our stress and suffering comes from being angry at life, angry at others, angry at God, and angry at ourselves for something that happened in the past. This is a waste of our precious energy. Such railing against what is doesn't change a thing and only makes us and everyone around us miserable.

We don't have to be miserable. There is another choice, and that is to accept what is and what has happened. This may seem difficult—even impossible. And for the ego, it is. But once we really get how irrational and ineffective our arguing with life is, we can learn to accept what is and what has happened. We can learn to align with the place within us that is accepting rather than with the place that isn't.

Not accepting something is actually a much more difficult road than accepting something. But to accept something, we have to be willing to let go of our anger and old ways of relating to life. We are here to discover that our suffering is optional. We can choose the stance we take toward life. The stance that produces less stress and suffering is always the best choice.

Strong Opinions

We all have opinions. The ego loves opinions because they give it a sense of knowing and of being right, even when it doesn't know and isn't right. Pretending to know is satisfying enough to the ego. Have you ever noticed how quickly you form an opinion about something, even with very little information about it? Most of our opinions are formed this way. Notice this process when it's happening. This is the ego at work performing one of its jobs, which is to create and maintain an identity as a particular person. Forming opinions is one of the ways the ego creates the false self.

Opinions are part of our identity, part of how we define ourselves: "I'm a Democrat, a vegan, a Christian, an environmentalist, a Conservative, a terrorist." Behind these identities lie opinions and other beliefs, all of which give us a sense of who we are. This is often why we're attached to our opinions and hold them so strongly: Who would we be without our opinions? Good question.

As long as we're human we will have beliefs and opinions, and there's nothing wrong with them. However, if we hold our opinions, no matter what they are, very strongly and rigidly and are unable to appreciate the complexity of issues and other points of view, we'll feel stressed-out whenever our opinions are challenged or we encounter those with different viewpoints.

Holding a position rigidly doesn't feel good. The body gets tense and takes a fighting stance toward those who see things differently. This sense of separation from others is painful. We may enjoy having opinions, because the ego likes having them, but notice how you feel emotionally and physically when you're holding an opinion unbendingly or expressing it vehemently. Our bodies don't like our strong opinions, which create stress in the body, not to mention stress in others. The antidote to this stress is to notice the effect that holding your opinions rigidly and expressing them forcefully has on your body and your relationships.

While the ego is at odds with others about their differences, our true self is curious, open, and interested in how others think and feel and why they think and feel as they do. If we can bring this curiosity to our sharing of opinions and beliefs with others and not assume that we have all the answers, we can enjoy exchanging ideas with others. We may even learn something from those with different opinions and grow as a result. And if we want others to consider our beliefs, being open to and curious about theirs are prerequisites.

Where does the idea "I'm right" come from? We all think that what we think is right, and we're eager to set other people straight who don't agree with us. We're built to agree with our own thoughts, whether they're true or not. Knowing this can allow for more openness and curiosity toward other people's views and more discrimination about our own.

Here are some questions to help you examine the value of your beliefs:

❖ *What are some of the beliefs you hold that cause conflict with others?*

❖ *How did you come to believe what you believe?*

❖ *Is what you believe true? How do you know it's true?*

❖ *Do these beliefs work for you or not? Do they make you happier and more loving or the opposite?*

Do you want to keep believing what you believe? If not, just see and acknowledge that a belief isn't the whole truth or that it may even be a lie. Once we see that something isn't the whole truth, holding it more lightly becomes much easier. And once we see that something is a lie, we can't keep believing it.

Many of us who were around in the 1970s loved the TV show *All in the Family* and were outraged and amused at Archie Bunker's unapologetic bigotry. We would never feel or act that way, we said to ourselves. But aren't we just as sure about our views as he was about his? And doesn't this separate us from others just as surely?

Softening our views doesn't mean we have less integrity, but that we have the integrity to put our ego and beliefs in their proper place. Our beliefs aren't the whole truth and they aren't that important, certainly not more important than peace of mind and peace on this planet.

Thoughts About the Past

The egoic mind likes to think about the past. It especially likes replaying euphoric and upsetting events. Or it reminisces about the past and refines its memories and the story of *you* according to current perceptions. The mind also likes to consider what might have happened if you or someone else had said or done something different, spinning past events into a fantasy. And it loves analyzing what was said and done in the past and trying to understand and give meaning to it.

Thoughts about the past naturally arise within everyone. There's nothing wrong with them, so you don't need to try to shut them out or stop them, which would be impossible anyway. But it's good to be aware of when your thoughts about the past become stressful, because there really is no need to be involved with such thoughts. We don't need to think about the past and such thoughts don't usually serve us.

If you're enjoying thinking about the past, then the only problem with that is that it takes you out of the present moment and its richness. All of our egoic thoughts—the pleasant and the unpleasant ones—take us out of our present moment experience, and we miss out on fully experiencing real life as it is happening right now. When we are deeply and fully experiencing the present moment, we discover that a lot more is happening than we may have realized when we were lost in thought and, more importantly, we discover the beauty and joy of being alive.

Some thoughts do much more than just take us out of the present moment; they stir up negative feelings. They cause stress in the here and now. It was bad enough to feel bad in the past, why would we want to remember something that reignites those feelings? We don't really, but undigested experiences from the past, especially traumatic and other emotionally charged ones, come up because something about them needs to be seen, healed, and integrated.

The psyche brings certain memories and emotions into conscious awareness so that they can be properly chewed and digested. This is part of a natural healing process, which is often initiated by being triggered, or getting our buttons pushed. We need to know what to do with such memories and emotions, or this triggering is likely to reinforce the emotions rather than heal them. Thinking about the past can strengthen the emotions connected to a memory. Therein lies the problem.

It's stressful to have feelings that we don't want to have. I chose these words to make the point that the stress comes from not wanting to have or not wanting to feel certain feelings, not from the feelings themselves. As human animals, we are programmed to resist unpleasant emotions, just as we are programmed to resist and avoid pain. Furthermore, because most of us were taught that certain emotions are bad, having such feelings makes us feel bad about ourselves. We feel wrong for having certain feelings, when they are perfectly normal, perfectly human.

Resisting or rejecting whatever is true and real in the moment, such as an emotion, and feeling bad about having an emotion puts us in a state of contraction, of stress. If emotions are what's up, then we need to attend to them in healthy ways. Being present sometimes means being present to an emotion if that happens to be what's showing up in the here and now.

The unhealthy ways that we tend to respond to our emotions also cause stress: To try to fix our feelings, we might obsessively think about the past, which only creates more feelings. Or we might eat or drink too much or indulge in other addictive behaviors to try to numb, distract, or comfort ourselves. Or we might retell our story again and again, which keeps the old feelings alive. These reactions maintain and reinforce feelings rather than heal them.

Thoughts and feelings related to the past don't have to be stressful if we know how to be with them in a way that helps digest the past experience and heal the feelings. This is the purpose of the analysis of the past that happens in psychotherapy. Bringing the past into the present moment with the intention to examine and heal it, as is done in therapy, is very different from how most of us relate to our memories and the feelings they stir up. More will be said about how to digest past experiences and heal emotions in the next chapter.

Of the various types of thoughts about the past mentioned earlier, someone might argue that thoughts that attempt to understand and give meaning to the past are worth thinking. We all want to learn from the past, but is analyzing the past the way to do that? The truth is, we can't help but learn from the past. The past changes us, and we move forward differently based on what we learned. This learning is already within us, although we may not even realize what we learned or how we were changed by a particular event.

Do we need to put this learning into words or understand why we had a particular experience? Any understanding we put into words is after the fact. We learned something, and knowing what that was or why something happened isn't the learning but something we attach to what we already know deep inside.

The problem with analysis and attaching meaning to the events in our lives is that our conclusions might not be complete or even true. We need to be mindful of what we conclude about an event because our conclusions will likely shape our future behavior. What I like to say about beliefs is that if a belief or conclusion results in being more loving, accepting, and at peace with life, then keep it; if it does the opposite, discard it.

My point is not that there's anything wrong with gaining understanding or analyzing the past, but that understanding and analysis are often overrated and the power of life to teach us is often underrated or overlooked. The events in our life shape and change us. We evolve as a result of them. Thinking about and trying to analyze, reconstruct, or rewrite those events can lead to living in the past instead of being present.

Anything we need to learn from the past will arise intuitively as an insight or an "Aha!" in its own time. One of the ways life teaches us is through intuitive insights. All of a sudden, we just understand something and know it to be true. This kind of knowing feels very solid but can be difficult to put into words. On the other hand, the understanding that the egoic mind tries to come up with through thinking is limited and potentially erroneous. The mind doesn't know what we need to understand about the past, but our being does. And our being speaks to us intuitively, not through the mind.

So it turns out that thoughts about the past are not very useful, true, or functional. Is it useful to think about the past? What does it do for you? How does it make you feel? What or who does thinking about the past serve? When you really look, you discover that thinking about the past usually contracts you and only serves the ego and its desire to tell the story of *you*, the story of your false self. That story rarely coincides with what your deepest self would say.

Our memories don't even accurately reflect what happened in the past, as many studies have shown. For example, most witnesses to a crime can't correctly describe the person they saw committing the crime or what happened. There are often as many versions of an event as witnesses. So how can our memories, which aren't likely to be accurate and which change over time, be valuable?

Our unhappy memories hook us, like a scab that we can't leave alone, until those memories and the feelings attached to them are resolved. Dwelling on memories in the ways that we generally do doesn't heal them. The healing process begins by being present to those feelings with the intent to digest and heal them.

One of the reasons we may cling to a memory and the painful feelings attached to it is that we refuse to forgive ourselves or others for something that happened, as if keeping the memory and painful feelings alive is purposeful. But keeping the past alive this way stunts our growth, keeps the negative emotions in play, and doesn't serve anyone. Not forgiving is like dragging a dead corpse around. We can never actually enliven what was lost, only the memory of what was lost. Unfortunately, a memory can't bring us the joy we long for, only the sorrow.

The reason many of us have difficulty forgiving is that we believe that forgiving ourselves or others for something is the same as condoning the harm that was done. Or by withholding, we may be trying to punish ourselves or others. But not forgiving only keeps us stuck in our ego. We only hurt ourselves when we refuse to forgive. Withholding forgiveness accomplishes nothing and makes it more difficult to experience our heart, our goodness.

To move out of our ego and back into our being, our goodness, we need to forgive ourselves and others. Forgiveness keeps us a prisoner of the ego, a prisoner to the very thing that caused the harm in the first place. What good is that? Forgiveness is something we do for ourselves so that we can move on and begin to live and love again. Forgiveness allows love to flower again, and love is what life is all about. Forgiveness makes it possible to put the past behind us and live in the present again. The antidote to being stuck in the past is forgiving ourselves and others.

Fears and Worries

There are two kinds of fear: the instantaneous fear that we experience when something is immediately threatening us and the fear that comes from imagining a potential threat in the future. The first type arises suddenly in the body, often without any thoughts. This type of fear is functional, preparing our body for fight or flight. The other type of fear is mentally generated and dysfunctional. It's conjured up by the egoic mind and then felt in the body. Imagined fears show up whenever we wonder, "What if...?" What I'm addressing in this section are these imagined fears and worries, which are some of the most stressful thoughts we have.

Out of the ego's dissatisfaction come desires for things to be better or different: We want a better car, more money, a new house, a better body. There's nothing wrong with having such desires. If we can hold them lightly and flexibly and realize their relative unimportance, we won't suffer if these desires aren't met. However, if we believe that getting what we want is essential to our happiness and safety, then we become afraid and worried that we won't get what we want. Getting something becomes part of a larger story about what *I* need to have *my* life work out. Such stories are lies we tell ourselves. They are the ego's story, the ego's perspective.

Desires and fears go hand-in-hand. If we didn't feel we needed something to be better or different in order to be happy, our fears and worries would be few. For this reason, worries and fears are especially strong in challenging times, when we want our life to be very different from what it is.

We often feel at the mercy of our fears and worries. How can we not worry? How can we not be afraid? But those are the wrong questions, because we can't stop the mind from worrying or thinking fearful thoughts. This is just what minds do. What we can do is recognize that our fears and worries are the ego's natural response to life because it distrusts life, wants to control life, and wants life to be different than it is.

Fears and worries are such a normal part of being human that proposing that they aren't functional may seem really radical. Since everyone has fears and worries, it's easy to assume that we *should* have them and that we need them, that they actually serve us. But do they?

For example, let's say that you just lost your job. Do you need the fear that you won't find another job or that you won't be able to pay your mortgage? Do these fears help you find another job or pay your mortgage? More likely, they magnify any negative feelings you have about losing your job and contribute to an overall negative state of consciousness. This state only makes it more difficult to find the confidence, energy, intuitive guidance, and motivation you need to find another job. Fear and worries contract us, and that can't be helpful in finding solutions to our challenges.

Fears and worries are activated and aggravated by the ego's ongoing "Yes, but...": "Yes, but there are no jobs. Yes, but I'm fifty-five years old. Yes, but I'll have to retrain. Yes, but I can't deal with this now." The ego's job is to say, "Yes, but..." to life, to come up with potential negatives. The intent is to keep us safe, but does it?

Do you really need the egoic mind's help in solving your problems and facing your challenges? We need our intellect and our intuition, but we don't need the egoic mind's advice. Don't any new perspectives and a positive vision come from something other than the egoic mind, from something deeper within you that you feel or intuit and then put into words? The gold that lies within each of us is not mined in the egoic mind. These are questions that are worth answering for yourself. Here are a few other questions to contemplate:

❖ *What effect do your fears and worries have on your body?*

❖ *Do your fears and worries help you move in the world, or do they contract and confuse you?*

❖ *Do your fears predict what is going to happen, or are they just possibilities?*

❖ *Is it helpful to consider such possibilities?*

❖ *Does being aware of such possibilities keep you safe?*

❖ *These possibilities may have happened to someone at some point, but are they relevant to you right now, in this moment?*

❖ *Aren't your fears just possibilities about some future moment that doesn't even exist?*

The problem with our worries and fears is that they put us in is a less functional state. When we are contracted and stressed-out, we're less aware, less conscious, less intelligent, and less in touch with our innate wisdom. By deactivating the forebrain, stress takes us out of the sensory experience of the here and now, where our inner wisdom is accessed. Our fears keep us in the grip of the more primitive aspect of ourselves—the ego—and out of touch with our being, which innately knows how to move in the world.

The antidote to our fears and worries is being in the present moment, because we can't be in the moment and be absorbed in our fearful thoughts at the same time. These are mutually exclusive states of consciousness. Being lost in thought is the definition of not being present, and being present is not being lost in thought.

What happens when we drop out of our egoic mind is that we contact our being, and our being trusts life. Why does it trust life? Because our being *is* life. We are life, but that sense of being connected to all that is, is obscured by the sense of being a separate self. The ego gives us the sense of being cut off from life and going it alone in this big and scary world. But when we experience the being that we are, we know that all is well and unfolding as it needs to. We know that life is good and trustworthy. We know that every one of our experiences has served and is serving our growth and evolution. And we trust that we will find our way and that life will provide us with what we need.

All of this is hogwash to the ego, which depends on mental constructs, such as fears, worries, plans, fantasies, beliefs, opinions, and desires, to guide it through life. These are the forces that guide our life when we are listening to the egoic mind. Are these good guides? Is the ego wise? The egoic mind is like a computer that provides information, but computers and egos can't provide wisdom. Our conditioning can't even be relied on to provide correct information.

There is an intelligence behind life, and we are it. It's not located in our mind, although it uses our intellect. We are a vast field of consciousness within which our body-mind operates. The ego is just part of the human body-mind. The ego is the sense of being an individual, and this helps us function in the world. But we don't need the egoic mind. We don't need the ego's advice and guidance.

Once you really see this, you are free to experience how beautiful and amazing this life is. The ego's fears and worries spoil the potential joy in being alive in these bodies on this wondrous planet. When we stop believing that we need our fears and worries, we can begin to live and love, because fear blocks our heart. Fear prevents us from being in life with an open-hearted love and gratitude for the gift that life is.

Thoughts About Other People

You might not think that your thoughts about others are stressful until you begin to examine them more closely and notice how they contract you when you're thinking them. Thinking about others doesn't feel good! It's stressful. Thinking about others also often creates stress in our relationships because so many of our thoughts about others are judgmental and unkind. Our opinions about others are bound to seep into our relationships either subtly or not so subtly.

Thoughts about others fall into several categories:

❖ Thoughts about what they said or did in the past and how you felt about that;

❖ Thoughts about what you think they'll say or do, should say or do, or would like them to say or do;

❖ Thoughts about what they're doing or planning to do, how you feel about that, including your worries and fears, and what you'd like others to do; and

❖ Descriptions of others, evaluations and judgments about them, and what you like or don't like about them.

A common thread in these thoughts is *you:* how you feel about someone, what you think of someone, and how that person affects you and makes you feel.

Granted, some of our thoughts and words about others are a simple statement of fact, without any agenda on the part of the ego. But a fact can quickly turn into a judgment or story about someone if the ego gets hold of it. The egoic mind takes a statement of fact like "He's going back to school" and follows it with a story that expresses an opinion or analysis of the person: "He has such a hard time knowing what he wants to do." The more aware you become of your thoughts, the more transparent the ego's agenda becomes.

Underlying most thoughts about others is an agenda on the part of the ego to be superior or to be right by pretending to know something that someone else doesn't know. When the ego relates to others, it naturally wants to be one up, because this helps the ego feel safe. Judgments, evaluations, comparisons, analyses, and many of our other thoughts about others are often in service to finding fault with others and thereby bolstering our ego.

Although the drive to be right and superior is a protective mechanism on the part of the ego, this is actually an outdated way that we are wired, or programmed, since working together with others supports our survival more than being in competition with them. A competitive stance toward others doesn't actually help us survive but interferes with our creating bonds with them that do help us survive.

Another problem is that our judgments, evaluations, and analyses aren't necessarily true. Even if they were true, what good are they? Do your judgments and evaluations change anything? Do they improve your relationship? Are what others do any of your business? If you are someone's therapist, then evaluations and analyses have their place, but judging is the opposite of what therapists do to be helpful to their clients.

In any event, most of our thoughts about others are kept to ourselves, which is usually a good thing. So it's useful to examine whether our thoughts about others actually serve *us*. It's pretty obvious that most of these thoughts wouldn't serve the other person, since many are quite unkind. Given that, sharing our thoughts about someone with others generally isn't helpful either and falls in the category of gossip.

So who are these thoughts for? What is their purpose? How do they affect you when you think them? And how do they affect your relationships? What aspect of yourself enjoys thinking these thoughts? Notice the pleasure that the ego has in feeling right and superior. The funny thing is, this "pleasure" doesn't actually feel good but contracts us.

One of the biggest problems with our judgmental and unkind thoughts about others is that they can poison our relationships even when we keep them to ourselves. Thinking negatively about someone is bound to cause problems in our relationship with that person, because those thoughts become the lens through which we see that person.

This lens is narrow and never includes the whole truth. It filters out what doesn't fit our ideas about someone. For instance, if you see someone as selfish, you'll notice every time that person behaves selfishly and filter out or play down instances when he or she isn't behaving selfishly. Once the ego has drawn a conclusion about someone, it looks for evidence to uphold that conclusion so that it can continue to feel right. Since how we think about people affects how we respond to them, our thoughts about others are far from innocuous.

When we have a lot of opinions and judgments about someone, those thoughts make it more difficult to be present to that person. We bring our history with that person and all the ideas and images we have about him or her into the present moment. Those things color that moment, making it more difficult to respond freshly to that person. We end up not relating to the person in front of us but to our ideas and feelings about that person. When we do that, we are living in a virtual reality, not reality. That isn't particularly satisfying for anyone.

Many of our thoughts about others are opinions about what they should or shouldn't do. Notice how often your mind pretends to know what others should and shouldn't do, just as it pretends to know what you should and shouldn't do. Where does this voice come from? Is it really your voice, your truest wisdom, or the ego's knee-jerk reaction to others? Even if these shoulds aren't spoken, what or whom are these shoulds serving? Only the ego, which is pretending to know something about someone else.

What a burden it is to think that we know or to feel that we should know what everyone else should and shouldn't do. The ego isn't humble. It assumes it knows what others should and shouldn't do. But do you really know? This is not to say that you might not have some very good advice sometime for someone based on your experience or intuition. And it may be just the thing to share that if asked. But have you noticed that unsolicited advice usually isn't very well received?

Thinking about others is stressful because we don't really know what's best for them and because it's exhausting trying to figure this out. It really isn't our business to figure out what's best for others. It's for them to discover this themselves. Only if they ask us is it appropriate to get involved in their business.

The only exception to this may be our children, as they need our guidance when they're young, although it's not a given that we know what's best for them. In any event, our children don't need us to worry about them, judge them, define them, or tell stories about them.

I realize that the suggestion that you refrain from thinking about others may seem extreme, especially to parents of grown children. But once you realize that the purpose of our thoughts about others is usually to maintain the ego's sense of being superior, your energy can be freed up to invest in more meaningful and productive activities. We only have so much time and energy, so why spend it on thoughts that are useless, draining, and potentially damaging to your relationships?

What a relief it is to realize that we don't have to know what others should or shouldn't do. Other people know best what they need to do. The most we can do is offer others support in discovering that the answers are within them—if they ask us for that support. Letting go of our thoughts about others by not giving such thoughts our attention leaves us with so much more energy and availability to be present to life.

Ideas of Perfection

One of the biggest causes of stress and suffering is trying to live up to ideas of perfection and then failing, as we always will, because there is no such thing as perfection. How can we attain something that isn't real, that doesn't exist in reality? Perfection is a concept and, as such, only exists in our mind. It has no concrete existence, unlike a tree or a chair, for instance. Those things are real. We don't stand a chance of attaining any of the mind's concepts, especially one as lofty as perfection, because concepts aren't real.

Our ideas of perfection don't come from our true self but from our conditioning. We are conditioned to create a virtual reality through thought. This virtual reality includes made-up images of what we think our life should look like and what we want it to look like. We are programmed to create such images. We can't help it. It's what our mind does.

However, because these images have nothing to do with reality, they're bound to cause suffering. How can life ever match our imagination? How can we or life ever match the images of perfection concocted by the mind? What are the odds of doing that? One in a million? One in a billion? One in a zillion?

No matter how slim the odds are, hope for perfection springs eternal in our virtual reality generator—the mind. We long for the perfect spouse, the perfect children, the perfect job, the perfect appearance, and perfect, unending happiness. We long for what life can never deliver no matter how hard we try, no matter how smart we are, no matter how good we are, no matter how much we want what we want. To the egoic mind, reality is a rotten deal. The mind claims that reality can and should be different than it is, and that's a lie. As long as we believe what the mind says about reality, we'll suffer.

Our mind creates images of perfection—of how life, we, or others should be and how we want them to be—and then we suffer and rail at life, ourselves, or others for not living up to these images. We really believe that we can have life our way. We are programmed to believe that.

In truth, we are in control of very little, and our desire for reality to be different than it is, is impotent. However, one thing we *are* in control of that makes all the difference is our attention. We can give our attention to the egoic mind's lies and suffer, or we can give our attention to reality, to what's true and real here and now.

We think that we know what perfection is, but perfection is whatever our mind decides it is, and that can change in a nanosecond. Our ideas of perfection are not only unattainable because they're unreal and unrealistic, but simply because life doesn't work that way. Life is the way it is, and it doesn't shape itself to our ideas about how it should be or to our desires for it to be a certain way, which I'm sure you've noticed!

Many of us exhaust ourselves trying to live up to our ideas of perfection. We get stressed-out and expend a huge amount of energy trying to make life match what we think it should be, as if our happiness and survival depended on it. This, of course, is the ego's point of view. The ego truly believes we can't be happy unless we create the life we think we need and become the person we think we need to be.

Where did all these beliefs come from? We picked them up from our parents, teachers, friends, TV, and all the other people who are also programmed to think this way. It may never have dawned on us to question these beliefs, just as it rarely dawns on most people. We pursue perfection without questioning what we're doing or noticing the suffering that pursuing perfection is causing us and everyone around us.

Our ideas of perfection often relate to everything being beautiful, in order, in tip-top shape and to never making a mistake. Who can make that happen? Nevertheless, many of us are committed to die trying! The best we can do is to do our best at whatever needs to be done and whatever is worth doing while not wasting our energy on things that don't really matter or on trying to do the impossible: rearrange the material world, ourselves, or others to match our ideas of how things should be.

We set such high standards for ourselves, as if our every action was a competition to prove our worth. Meeting our ideas of perfection becomes a way of trying to prove our value as a human being and trying to overcome the feelings of inadequacy created by the ego. The ego is behind our ideas of perfection and the feelings of inadequacy that result when we don't meet its made-up goals.

This generation of ideas and feelings is taking place in our virtual reality and has nothing to do with real life. It's taking place internally. No one else would know that this was going on inside us except that they see us racing through life, stressed-out, and unhappy. Of course, since most people are doing the same thing, this seems normal. Around and around we go, trying to live up to our ideas of perfection, feeling inadequate because we can't, and then striving all the harder to prove our worth to ourselves.

Worth is also a concept. It's part of the ego's game of dividing the world into good and bad, which are just more concepts. There is no such thing as good or bad. In reality, things just are the way they are. No evaluation. No story. No drama. No winner, no loser. Do the trees have preferences? Does the sun refuse to shine because it's having a bad day? Reality is simple. It is what it is, neither good nor bad, neither right nor wrong.

From the perspective of our true self, life is perfect just the way it is. From the perspective of our true self, perfection is however life is and however we are in this moment. Life is as it is, and that's the way it's meant to be. You are as you are, and you are as you are meant to be for now, because in this moment you can't be any other way than the way you are. That's the truth. Why make being the way you are wrong? Why make life wrong? It's only the egoic mind that does this. Can you see how much more peaceful you would feel if you traded in the ego's truth for the real truth?

We were never meant to be anything other than the way we are right now. True perfection is life just as it is. We must learn to love and accept ourselves and others just as we are. We must learn to love reality and withdraw our attention from all of the unreal ideas that cause us to suffer. Why suffer? We create suffering and stress, and we can stop creating suffering and stress. We have that power.

∞

By this time, you probably realize that there aren't many thoughts that *don't* cause stress. The beauty is that we don't need any of these thoughts that cause stress. Here's a rule you can trust to always be true: If a thought causes stress, you don't need it. The reason you don't need stressful thoughts is that they come from the ego, and the ego isn't wise enough to run or guide your life. The ego pretends to be, and it may seem to be, but seeming doesn't make it so. That we think we need the thoughts that run through our mind to function, survive, and be happy is an illusion. The proof is that there are plenty of people who don't follow their egoic minds but something much deeper, which doesn't express itself through the voice in the head.

I invite you to examine how necessary and useful the thoughts that run through your mind are. And I challenge you to find a necessary thought. What you discover is that this chatter that we think of as our thoughts arises in our mind from nowhere, and much of it is silly, petty, illogical, confused, contradictory, ignorant, judgmental, dissatisfied, and unkind. At best, on a good day, it's neutral or friendly and upbeat.

How wonderful it is that this senseless and often unpleasant chatter doesn't actually belong to us. It's just part of the human condition. These are the same kinds of thoughts that all human beings have and suffer over. These thoughts are the cause of suffering, not the cure. When we stop looking to the egoic mind for solutions to our so-called problems (the ones dreamed up by the mind) and turn our attention to real life as it is happening here and now, we discover that any solutions, guidance, insights, wisdom, and motivation that we need arise naturally out of the flow.

We never did need the ego to tell us how to live our life or motivate us or even help us survive. The being that we are has been living our life all along. There's no one else here but this being! It has allowed us to be run by the egoic mind—until we wake up to the truth about the mind. If we are willing to set aside the only thing that obscures the beautiful being that we are—the egoic mind—our being will shine and express itself through us more fully. The being that we are knows how to live life peacefully, lovingly, and happily.

The egoic mind is the generator of stress, and when we stop allowing it to dominate our awareness, stress ceases or greatly diminishes. What makes many of the thoughts that run through our mind stressful is that they result in emotions to one extent or another, the kind of emotions we don't like to have. How we deal with these emotions often causes problems in our life and consequently more stress.

Fear, anger, guilt, shame, resentment, envy, hatred, jealousy are universally experienced as unpleasant. We, as humans, are programmed to resist feeling anything unpleasant, so we do any number of things to avoid feeling these emotions or to get rid of the feelings themselves: We repress or deny them; act them out in damaging ways; try to change whatever caused them; or cope with them with drugs, food, alcohol, or compulsive shopping.

We do these things instead of just being with the feeling as it's being experienced, which calms it and allows it to naturally relax into another experience. Essentially, we're afraid of our feelings and try to manage them in ways that cause them to continue to be a problem for us. Just sitting with a feeling and neither repressing it nor acting on it is counter our natural tendencies.

The trouble with handling feelings in our usual ways is that the feeling either festers underground, only to rear its head some other time, or is reinforced as we express it in the usual ways, often by acting out unkindly. If we naturally expressed our feelings in healthy ways, expressing them wouldn't be a problem. But our knee-jerk reactions are usually hurtful to ourselves and others, since most of our feelings get expressed angrily, even our hurt. Anger is destructive to our relationships. Anger is also destructive to our sense of self, because it's difficult to feel good about ourselves when we're angry a lot.

Unfortunately, letting our anger take over reinforces and strengthens the tendency to express our feelings this way. So the more we do this, the harder it is to not do this or to express our feelings more constructively. The more power we give the egoic mind to wreck havoc with our life, the more powerful it becomes and the more difficult it is to ignore and detach from.

Whether emotions are repressed, denied, acted out, or numbed by addictive behaviors, they take a toll on the body. So although it's natural to have emotions and it's natural to want to avoid them or express them destructively, it behooves us to learn better ways of dealing with them. If we can become more conscious of the thoughts that tend to create unpleasant emotions, such feelings won't be created in the first place. Or, at the very least, these feelings won't be acted out so unconsciously and therefore reinforced. Then the cycle of reacting emotionally to life can begin to be broken.

Imagine how much less stressful your life and relationships would be if events and people didn't stir up unpleasant emotions. Fortunately, we have some control over our emotional state, in that we can learn to relate to our stressful thoughts in a way that diffuses their power and therefore their ability to make us feel bad.

The next chapter explores what to do when unpleasant feelings do show up, as they naturally will. Feelings don't have to be a problem. It's what we do with them that causes problems. Learning how to relate to your feelings and to the thoughts that tend to create them will make it easier for you to glide gracefully through life, without all the stress and drama caused by being at the mercy of your emotions.

CHAPTER 3

Working With Stressful Thoughts and Feelings

Your Thoughts and Feelings Aren't Yours

Stressful thoughts and feelings happen, and they seem to be *our* stressful thoughts and feelings. As long as they feel like ours—as long as we're identified with them and believing them—then our stressful thoughts and feelings take us for a ride. We can get off this ride and into a different relationship to our thoughts and feelings by recognizing that they are part of our humanness, part of the human condition, and not a reflection of who we really are.

Our thoughts and feelings don't belong to us. We didn't put them there or create them. It would be more accurate to say that they belong to all of humanity. Thoughts and feelings come with being alive. They are part of the human animal, part of the body-mind that we operate through. We are not the body-mind or our thoughts and feelings but that which animates the body-mind and uses it as a vehicle to experience this glorious world of form. Yet, we are programmed to experience our thoughts and feelings as *ours*.

As part of this programming, there seems to be a person who is having a thought or a feeling, but where is that person? Is that person your body? Your mind? Your personality? Is that who you are? Who is having the thought or feeling? Who is this *you* that you think of as yourself? Where is it located?

When you look, you can't find a person who is having a thought or feeling. Although thoughts and feelings are occurring in what you call your body-mind, there is no person having them. This person is illusory. There is no person, only an idea of a person. This illusory person is the false self, which is why it's called false. It doesn't actually exist. It exists only as an idea or a group of ideas about oneself. Who you *think* you are is only a set of ideas about who you think you are.

Thoughts and feelings arise in our body-mind out of nowhere. When they arise and we identify with them, we feel like they're ours, like we came up with them. But we didn't. They aren't personal. They aren't ours. With this recognition comes some freedom to choose not to believe these thoughts, which are often stressful, and so become free of the stress they cause.

To have a different relationship to our thoughts and feelings than the one we were programmed with, which is to believe our thoughts and feelings and to get our identity from them, we have to first see that our thoughts and feelings aren't ours and do not define us. And then we have to keep remembering this in every moment. We're talking about seeing through what is our deepest, most pervasive conditioning — the programming that causes us to feel separate, lacking, and in competition with life rather than at one with life.

When this programming is thoroughly seen through and no longer believed, we are not left with nothing. Moving beyond this programming moves us beyond our greatest limitation and the cause of suffering, and what we're left with is joy, love, and the essence of our being. This programming is the only thing keeping us from the deeper happiness and loving nature of our true being. So when this programming is seen through, we're left with everything we have ever wanted and stripped of everything we never needed but thought we did.

How can we be convinced that we don't need the thoughts broadcasted by the egoic mind? This is no easy task, as the thoughts themselves lead us to believe we'll be lost without them. The illusion of the false self is a tricky one! If the illusion weren't a clever one, it would be seen through much more easily. But it's not. The challenge is to stop trusting our egoic mind and begin to trust something else that is more subtle and yet much more real than thoughts.

Our true being is here living this life and always has been the only thing living this life, yet all the while, we have supposed ourselves to be someone or something else. We mistook the character and the roles we are playing for our true identity. But it's time now for many of us to recognize that we are much more than this character and that our being has just allowed us to believe we were this character.

The way this ruse was perpetrated and is maintained was by programming us to believe that our thoughts were our thoughts. Believing these thoughts caused us to be a certain way in life; they caused us to respond and react in the various ways our character does: If our thoughts define us as a victim, we feel like a victim and behave like one. If our thoughts define us as incompetent, we feel incompetent, and that may be a self-fulfilling prophecy. If our thoughts say we have reason to be afraid, we feel afraid. If our thoughts push us to hurry and get a lot done, we do that and get stressed-out.

If we believe our thoughts, then they define us and determine our experience of life, how we feel, and what we do. We are, in many respects, a puppet to our conditioning, to our thoughts and feelings—when we believe them. When we are identified with them and believe them, we are at the mercy of them. They run the show.

If our thoughts were benevolent, wise, trustworthy, and good guides for how to live, then believing them would lead to a very different life than what our programming generally leads to. To discover the nature, truth, and value of this programming, just notice the results of following it in your own life, in other people's lives, in our society, and in our world. If our programming were benevolent and wise, we would be happy, loving, and at peace, or at least more so, and there would be no need to seek greater peace.

When you become very familiar with your thoughts and begin to question and examine them, you discover that they are:

- ❖ A jumble of useful, useless, true, untrue, and contradictory information;

- ❖ Beliefs, judgments, and opinions, many of them unfounded;

- ❖ Desires, wishes, hopes, likes and dislikes, fears, and worries;

- ❖ Simple observation and commentary about whatever is being experienced.

Yes, our thoughts contain some helpful information, but they contain little else that is needed or helpful, and I would even argue that the helpful information is something we already know and don't need to be reminded of by our thoughts. When our identities and actions are based on such thoughts, is it any wonder that so many people have lives that are full of stress, drama, confusion, and disappointment? When I first realized this about my thoughts, I was stunned that I hadn't seen this sooner.

Once we begin to really look at what the egoic mind tells us day after day (which tends to be much the same), it becomes obvious that we've been following a false master. Fortunately, there's a better way to live, a truer way, and we are meant to discover that. The way to do that is by first seeing the truth about your thoughts, which is something you have to see for yourself. You have to do this investigation yourself moment by moment as you live your life, and nothing—no amount of reading or study—can take the place of this investigation.

A New Relationship to Thoughts and Feelings

When we change our relationship to our thoughts, our relationship to our feelings will also change. This new relationship to thoughts is one of noticing your thoughts and then recognizing them for what they are. Sometimes this is easy—you instantly see the falseness, uselessness, or ridiculousness of a thought and you let it go. At other times, this isn't so easy. Some thoughts have a number of feelings attached to them, which makes those thoughts especially "sticky" and difficult to not believe. As a result, some thoughts are very difficult to let go of.

Thoughts and feelings that are very convincing have to be investigated carefully and often repeatedly before they lose their hold on us and we are able to let them go. For instance, those who grew up with abuse or without the proper nurturing often strongly feel and believe that they are unlovable. Thoughts and feelings such as these need careful and deep examination, usually with the help of a professional, before they are no longer believed. This can be difficult work, but it is important work, because such thoughts and feelings shape and limit us, often much more than we realize.

The new relationship to thoughts and feelings that is possible is one of recognizing and accepting them as part of the human condition but realizing that they don't define us or say anything at all about who we really are. Isn't it great that the petty, angry, judgmental, unkind, and discontent individual that our thoughts often make us out to be isn't who we really are and that we can move beyond feeling and behaving in these destructive ways? Our true self is inherently good, kind, and in love with life.

Isn't that what we all really want, to be our best self instead of our worst self? Well, the good news is that we really are our best self and not our worst self, since the worst self is created and maintained solely by believing our negative thoughts and acting out the negative feelings that come from those thoughts.

Thoughts and feelings arise within all human beings, and they are very similar from one human being to the next. The stressful thoughts and feelings that you have are nearly the same as the ones I and everyone else has. We are all in the same boat as human beings, and no on escapes this fate. And yet, it's also possible to become free of the domination of such thoughts and feelings.

Even enlightened or spiritually awakened people have stressful thoughts, but they've realized the truth about their thoughts and so are free to have something else determine their experience of life. They've learned to live as their true self within this human life. And so can you. The secret that these individuals know and have known throughout history is now available to all who are ready to receive it.

The skills, or steps, for becoming established in a new relationship to thoughts and feelings are:

1. Notice stressful thoughts and feelings,

2. Allow and accept stressful thoughts and feelings,

3. Let go of stressful thoughts and feelings,

4. Investigate stressful thoughts and feelings that you're unable to let go of,

5. Reframe stressful thoughts if you need to, and

6. Be with stressful feelings if that's called for.

Obviously, to become free of our stressful thoughts and feelings, we first have to be aware of what we are thinking and feeling. Sometimes awareness alone is enough to dis-identify from and let go of a thought or feeling and be free of the stress it's causing. Awareness gives us a little distance from a thought or feeling, a little objectivity. For example, I might be hurrying around and feeling stressed-out, but as soon as I become aware of the "hurry up" voice and the tension in my body, that awareness might interrupt my behavior enough to allow me to see that I need to slow down. Then if I do slow down, that would put an end to feeling stressed-out.

With some stressful thoughts and feelings, however, more than just becoming aware of them and then letting them go may be needed to dis-identify from them. Sometimes we have to spend a little time with a stressful thought or feeling, acknowledging it, accepting it, letting it be there, and experiencing it fully without resisting it or pushing it away, before we can come out from under its spell, because it may be that we need to discover more about it. In the previous example, if I hadn't been able to stop hurrying because unconsciously I was afraid that something bad would happen if I slowed down, then taking the time to realize that I was afraid of that might be enough to calm the fear and allow me to continue more peacefully. If that realization wasn't enough to calm the fear, then staying with that fear a little longer and investigating it further would probably be necessary to dispel the sense that I needed to hurry.

Allowing and accepting a stressful thought or feeling is often necessary before we can let it go. Allowing and accepting it also gives the thought or feeling space and time to be there and opens the door to experiencing it fully and discovering something more about it, if that is what is needed before we are able to let it go. Without first allowing a stressful thought or feeling to be there, how can we investigate it? And if we don't accept it, why would we be willing to investigate it? Allowing and accepting a stressful thought or feeling makes it possible to have a new relationship to it, one that is neither identified with the thought or feeling nor pushing it away, but curious about it and open to it and to finding out more about it.

When we stop being identified with a stressful thought or feeling and fall back into the Witness in relationship to it, it stops feeling like *my* thought or *my* feeling, and it becomes just *a* thought or feeling. It's more like humanity's thought or feeling rather than ours personally. Paradoxically, dis-identification makes it possible to relate to our stressful thoughts and feelings more intimately than when we were identified with them, because if they aren't ours, then we don't need to resist them or push them away.

When we no longer think a thought or feeling is bad or that it means something bad about us, then we won't feel the need to run from or reject it. This is why accepting our thoughts and feelings is so important. Acceptance counteracts our natural inclination to reject a stressful thought or feeling and allows for the possibility of dis-identification and investigation, which leads to freedom from that piece of conditioning.

These first two steps—being aware of a thought or feeling and allowing and accepting it—are key to moving beyond the conditioning that limits us, makes us feel bad, and creates unnecessary stress in our life. The next sections describe in greater detail these two skills, or steps, and several others, such as letting go, investigation, reframing, and how to be with a feeling, all of which are necessary for a new relationship to our stressful thoughts and feelings.

Noticing Stressful Thoughts and Feelings

Noticing is a profound spiritual practice in itself because it gets us in touch with what is noticing and experiencing life, with Consciousness, our true self. Consciousness notices; it is what witnesses and experiences life. It is who we are. Whenever we do what our being naturally does, we align with it. For instance, if we say something compassionate to ourselves or to someone else, we align with our true nature because our true nature is compassionate. Or if we accept ourselves or someone else, we align with our true nature because our true nature is accepting. Or if we notice our experience and fully experience it, we align with our true nature because our true nature is what is aware and experiencing life.

Buddhists call this practice of noticing, *mindfulness*. Being mindful means being aware of our present moment experience, including our thoughts, feelings, intuitions, internal experiences, bodily sensations, sounds, sights, and other sensory input. In any moment, a lot is going on, and it's all in flux. So there's always plenty to notice in our present moment experience. The present moment is alive with activity and experience.

Most people are aware of only a fraction of what they're thinking, since many thoughts come and go so quickly as to be relatively unconscious even though they are technically in our conscious awareness. We can't possibly be aware of all of the thoughts that fly through our mind, and we don't need to be. But it's useful to be aware of or to become aware of the ones that create negative feelings and cause us to suffer.

Even when they are aware of their thoughts and feelings, most people don't tend to examine or question them. Nevertheless, many are waking up from the egoic trance and becoming more aware of their thoughts and the effect that their thoughts have on their lives and choosing more consciously to let go of the thoughts that don't serve them. This is a huge step in the emotional evolution of our species.

What is it that wakes up and becomes more conscious of the programming and of thoughts? What is it that notices the programming and thoughts, can evaluate the thoughts, and can choose to move in a different way than one's thoughts suggest? There's something here that is wiser and more discerning than these thoughts, and that is who we really are.

What notices and discerns is the true self. The true self is the consciousness that makes it possible to experience life. This Consciousness is a great mystery because it can only be described by how it is experienced, since it isn't a thing apart from everything else. The wisdom traditions say that this Consciousness is all-pervading and behind and within all creation, although it isn't important that you believe that.

More important than any belief is the experience of the consciousness that is here right now, experiencing these words and their impact and experiencing anything else that is being experienced. This consciousness is the most fundamental truth of existence. The one thing you can know for sure about yourself is

"I am." How do you know you exist? You are conscious. You experience.

How funny it is that a false self exists at all, since we don't need it. We need an ego to give us the sense of being a particular individual so that we can function as the character we are meant to play, but we don't need the egoic mind to define us and tell us how to live this life. We can still be this character without listening to the limiting and negative programming that comes through the egoic mind. The false self and its limiting programming is the illusion that we are meant to shed at some point in our evolution. But until we begin to see through this illusion, believing that we are the false self is exactly the experience we are meant to have.

What wakes up out of the false self and sees the truth about egoic thoughts is Consciousness, which was temporarily lost in the experience of being a suffering self. We all eventually discover that suffering is optional, as we learn to dis-identify with the ideas and beliefs in the egoic mind that create the false self who suffers, and we begin to more fully embody our true identity.

Of key importance in this awakening process is the strengthening of our ability to be aware, conscious, and centered in our present moment experience. Usually this happens as a result of some spiritual practice, particularly through meditation. This can also happen by learning to concentrate the mind in present moment experience some other way, as artists, musicians, dancers, or athletes do when they're engaged in their artistry.

Being fully present in the moment is an experience of our true nature. The more time we spend being present, the easier it is to be present and remain present and the more familiar we become with our true nature and its way of being in the world. Certain pathways in the brain are developed by meditation and other practices that bring us into present moment awareness. So, like any skill, we have to practice being in present moment awareness to get better at it; hence, the emphasis on spiritual practice in so many spiritual traditions. How this is relevant to becoming more aware of thoughts and feelings is that this, too, is something we need to practice and something that is developed through spiritual practices and by being present.

I like to call Consciousness the Noticer because Consciousness is very much experienced as that which notices and experiences. The Noticer is a fitting term because it's so neutral, like Consciousness. One of the qualities of our true nature besides being aware is that it is allowing and accepting. "Noticing" captures how consciousness touches the experiences of life but doesn't push them away, cling to them, judge them, or even evaluate them as good or bad, which are all features of the egoic self.

What we are is often also called Awareness, since that word also captures the neutrality of our true self and the experience of our true self—it is aware. This Awareness is just that, without evaluation, judgment, or liking or disliking whatever it is aware of. It embraces everything equally.

Although Consciousness isn't judgmental, it is discerning and naturally moves toward what is true for it and away from what is not true for it in any moment. This discernment isn't accompanied by a mental discussion of the pros and cons and potential outcomes of moving one way or another, it just moves.

So when we are in touch with who we are, we naturally move in certain directions, often without much thought or rationale for doing so, which is so unlike the egoic state of consciousness. Every one of us experiences this natural and spontaneous response of Consciousness to life in many moments during the day without thinking much about this. It's how our being moves through life.

Once we understand the value of becoming more aware of our sensory experience and of what we're thinking and feeling and of everything else that is happening in our present moment awareness, that alone increases the likelihood that we will be more aware. Valuing being more aware and making an intention to be more aware are the first steps in becoming more aware of our thoughts and feelings.

We can also strengthen this intention by doing certain things, such as stating this intention aloud or in writing and asking for help in becoming more aware in the form of a prayer. And if we follow up this intention with a practice of meditation or some other spiritual practice, we'll not only be developing the skill we need to be more aware, but we'll be reinforcing our intention with our actions.

Something else you may want to do to help you become more aware of your thoughts and feelings is to make a list of the things your egoic mind says to you. Set aside a day to take a little time to notice your thoughts and write some of them down. Then spend some time with this list and ask yourself a few questions:

❖ What types of thoughts are on this list? For example, are they judgments, shoulds, complaints, desires, fantasies, memories, likes, opinions, fears, worries, self-doubt, or about time?

❖ Which types of thoughts are most prevalent?

❖ Then examine individual thoughts:

- Is it true?

- How does that thought affect me if I believe it?

- Is that thought helping me live this life? Do I need that thought? Could I live without it? Is it useful?

Here's a list of some of my mental commentary:

I wish I didn't have to get up.

It's raining.

I can't believe I said that.

That party won't be any fun.

That is so lame!

I hate sweeping the patio.

I wish I didn't have to walk the dogs today.

What do I need to do now?

He always does that.

What do I feel like eating?

I would never do that.

I wonder what she thinks of me.

I don't feel very good.

I think I've gained some weight.

I wonder what my brother is doing today.

She shouldn't do that.

I love cantaloupe.

It's hard to pick out a good watermelon.

I can't imagine doing that.

I shouldn't eat all of this.

What a bitch I am!

I don't know how to answer that email.

I'm bummed out because my wrist hurts.

What should I do tomorrow?

Yikes! I'm getting old.

What time is it?

What should I wear today?

I'm tired.

I'm hungry.

I'd better get going.

These are the types of things that run through my mind on a regular basis. I'm hard-pressed to find anything of value in this list. Do I need the thought "It's raining" to know it's raining? Or "I'm hungry" to know that I'm hungry? These thoughts and so many others on this list merely put into words what I'm already experiencing and pretend to be telling me something I don't already know.

Do I really know that a party won't be fun just because I have that thought? I've discovered from experience that my mind's assumptions are often wrong, although an assumption like the one about a party could be a self-fulfilling prophesy or keep me from going to the party and finding out what it would have been like.

After asserting what I think someone or something is going to be like, I often say, "But life loves to make a fool out of me," acknowledging how often I'm wrong in believing I know something that I don't. Is it helpful to pretend this way? It's really fine that the egoic mind does this, because it was built to do this.

But it's good to realize that the egoic mind doesn't actually know most of what it claims to know.

Are thoughts expressing likes and dislikes useful? Everyone has likes and dislikes, and such thoughts arise in our egoic mind numerous times during the day. Maybe if you're at a melon stand, faced with an assortment of melons, the thought "I love cantaloupe" might be relevant. But, then again, at that moment you don't really need that thought to pick out a melon. Without that thought, wouldn't you just pick out the kind of melon you liked anyway?

Most of our thoughts are simply commentary about what we're already doing and experiencing, what we did or experienced in the past, and what we might do or want to do or experience in the future. Meanwhile, the being that we are goes about life, picking out melons, getting something to eat when we're hungry, resting when we're tired, and doing everything else we do. Our thoughts often influence these activities, but if we didn't follow these thought or didn't have them, we would still pick out a melon, eat, rest, and do all the other things we do to support our existence.

The egoic mind takes credit for running the show called *my life*, but what's actually happening is that who we really are just allows the egoic mind to add its input and take credit for the show. This is why the ego is called the false self—because it's false, it's a phony. It's not real but, rather, just thoughts that pretend to know and pretend to be somebody.

This might be a good place to mention one kind of thought that *is* useful: intuitions or inspirations that pop into the mind. They might be a reminder to do something, a creative idea, an insight, or even a warning. For example, many years ago, I was at a stoplight, and as it turned green, I heard in my mind, "Look left." When I did that, I saw a car barreling through the intersection. Without this warning, I'm not sure I would have seen that car.

I would classify these types of thoughts as intuitions and inspirations from our being, not the usual egoic mind chatter. When they land in the mind, there's a feeling of expansion and "Aha!" which is unlike how we experience our egoic mind. These thoughts have a different quality to them than our usual mental commentary. Because of this qualitative difference, they stand out from the egoic thoughts. So we don't need to be concerned that we'll miss these inspired thoughts if we ignore the egoic chatter. In fact, if we are lost in the egoic trance, we're more likely to miss or dismiss these special thoughts than catch them.

After many years of practicing meditation and mindfulness, I don't believe most of the thoughts that run through my mind. I experience my thoughts as a voice in my head, one that often complains. Complaints seem to be some of my character's favorite thoughts. We all have certain favorites. I'm not particularly bothered by the complaints, judgments, and other negative thoughts in my mind, although sometimes they catch me up and I give voice to them. But even as they're coming out of my mouth, I don't really believe them and can feel their hollowness and lack of truth. And yet, if someone is around, they might get expressed. Thankfully, the thoughts that run through my mind have become more neutral, less negative, and easier to dismiss and not express. If I'm feeling particularly good, my thoughts are much more upbeat but still not useful or interesting.

The only caveat to the practice of noticing our thoughts and feelings is that unless we also notice our sensory experience, we can get caught up in our internal experiences and not be fully present to everything else that's being experienced in the moment. Too much emphasis on noticing thoughts and other internal experiences, which may be necessary when we first start a practice of noticing, or mindfulness, can lead to solely watching our thoughts and not being present to the rest of life. When we are noticing only our thoughts, our nose is still glued to the television set of our egoic mind even though we're not identified with the thoughts anymore.

This doesn't leave us much more present to reality than when we were identified with those thoughts and the ongoing movie in our mind. Nevertheless, this is often what happens before we learn to be more completely established in the present moment, which would include being fully in our body and senses as well as noticing the coming and going of our thoughts and other internal experiences.

The practice of noticing as it applies to our stressful thoughts and feelings often needs to be more than just briefly noticing a stressful thought or feeling and then moving on, although that might be enough to dis-identify with some stressful thoughts or feelings. But if we still believe a stressful thought or feeling and can't let go of it, then it's likely that there are other unconscious or semi-conscious beliefs and feelings that are behind the stressful thought or feeling and holding it in place. When that's the case, we also need to notice and fully experience the feeling in our body and everything connected to it, such as any resistance to it, beliefs, and other feelings.

Many of our stressful beliefs that were established a long time ago, such as "I'm not loveable" or "I'm not worthy of happiness," aren't clearly articulated in our ongoing mental commentary but lie just beneath the surface and often come to the surface when we're under stress (e.g., "I'm so stupid. Why can't I do anything right!"). Since these unconscious or semi-conscious beliefs are what generate many of our negative feelings, we can uncover these more elusive beliefs by fully experiencing a feeling energetically in our body and investigating it. Our negative feelings are actually a blessing, because without them and the possibility of investigating them, many of our stressful beliefs would remain buried and running us unconsciously. Thus, noticing is the first step to becoming free of not only our conscious beliefs but our unconscious ones.

For example, let's say you notice that you're angry. Sometimes just noticing anger is enough to not get more involved in it and for it to simply dissipate naturally. But if anger persists or is recurring, then fully experiencing it energetically in the body and noticing the thoughts and other feelings related to it is called for. Staying with a feeling energetically and investigating it in this way is likely to reveal some mistaken beliefs that caused the anger, such as, "He shouldn't have done that to me," as well as other feelings, such as hurt or sadness. Perhaps the hurt and sadness harken back to another time in your life when someone else did something hurtful to you. Realizing the source of our feelings is often enough to heal them.

Practices and Explorations

1. As you go about your day, notice your energetic state. Notice whether you feel contracted and tense or at peace, expanded, and in the flow. Your state may be anywhere on a continuum between extremely contracted to extremely expanded and at peace. Most people spend most of the time somewhere in the middle. When you feel contracted, ask, "What am I believing or telling myself that's causing me to feel contracted?" It could be more than just one thing. Once you recognize the source of the contraction, the contraction will most likely relax.

2. Think of something that causes you to feel stressed-out. How do you experience this stress in your body? What thoughts accompany this state? Stay with this experience a while with acceptance and curiosity. Now, notice how you feel when you think a grateful, kind, loving, or accepting thought. Really explore the difference between these two states and experiment with this some more.

Allowing and Accepting Stressful Thoughts and Feelings

Doing anything other than allowing and accepting the stressful thoughts and feelings that show up keeps those thoughts and feelings around in our body-mind and makes it more likely that they'll show up again with just as much strength.

What we generally do with stressful thoughts and feelings is spin around in our mind trying to fix them with more thoughts, which only creates more feelings and keeps us tethered to the egoic state of consciousness. Or we might get angry at them or try to push them away, which results in tension in our body—stress—and does nothing to change or transform the stressful thoughts or feelings.

To transform these stressful energies, we have to be willing to experience them energetically in our body and take a look at them. For that, we have to let the stressful thought or feeling be there just as it is so that we can explore it and find out about it. If we don't allow it to be there, we won't discover anything about it, particularly if it is true.

Stressful thoughts are stressful because they aren't true. They aren't the most complete truth but a partial truth, and a partial truth is actually a lie. For instance, if you said, "I can't do anything right," you'd be lying because you'd be leaving out all the times when you did do something right. Besides, what is "right" anyway? It's just a concept, a made-up idea or belief.

The fact that stressful thoughts contract us is life's way of pointing out their lack of truth or completeness. Life also points out the truth of something by expanding and relaxing us when we think it or speak it. For example, when you say, "All is well" and you believe that, you relax and feel at ease, because the truth is that all is well from the perspective of our being. It is a universal truth, although not one that our ego buys into.

Many people who discover that the ego is the troublemaker, which it is, become angry when they realize their egoic thoughts keep coming. They go to battle with the ego. They want it to die. But battling and being angry at egoic thoughts won't make them go away. Doing this is called resistance, and as the saying goes, "What we resist persists." The only approach that can lessen the strength and possibly the number of egoic thoughts is letting the thoughts be there and accepting that they are there but not feeding them with more thoughts.

You've probably noticed that thoughts just pop into your mind, and you've probably realized that you can't do anything about that. However, at the point that a thought arises, if you are aware of it and don't automatically identify with it or get upset about having that thought, you can either choose to agree with it ("That's what *I* think!") and continue down that thought-train or choose to not jump on that thought-train by just allowing that thought to be there but not giving it your attention and not actively thinking about it.

A practice of meditation helps us become more aware of our thoughts and lengthens this space of time before identification happens, which is the difference between suffering and freedom from suffering. The longer this space of time is, the easier it is to not identify with a thought. A longer space of time breaks the egoic trance and gives us a chance to see a thought for what it is. The more time we have to observe a thought, the easier it is to see through it—to see it's falseness and to see how buying into it won't serve us.

Allowing and accepting a stressful thought is important because it lengthens that space of time and makes it much more possible and likely that we won't identify with that thought. It's paradoxical that allowing and accepting a stressful thought actually makes it possible to dis-identify with it, release us from the stress of it, and ultimately heal it. Allowing and accepting a thought doesn't mean agreeing with it, however, which is what we are doing when we identify with a thought.

Accepting something you don't like, whether it's a feeling, a state of mind, or an external condition, can seem really hard, and many struggle with this. How do you accept being sick or depressed or lonely or financially strained or confused? How do you accept being afraid about getting old or being angry at your ex-spouse or having done something terrible to someone? Accepting such things can seem like resignation or submission or like you're condoning them without doing anything to change them. But accepting something just means that you're willing to let it to be as it is. You accept that it is the way that it is. Accepting is allowing it to be the way it already is.

Accepting a stressful thought or feeling may seem like it would keep the thought or feeling around and make it difficult to change it, which isn't generally what we want. But, paradoxically, accepting something we don't like actually makes it easier to transform what we don't like, and it is the secret to healing difficult emotions.

The reason this is so is that accepting makes it possible for the situation or the stressful thought or feeling to naturally evolve, as it will if we fully see and experience it. We inhibit our own evolution and the evolution of our stressful thoughts and feelings when we reject what we're experiencing and push it out of our awareness.

Thoughts and feelings, and even situations and conditions, have a lifespan and course that they are following. If we allow whatever is to be as it is, it will evolve to the next stage. But if we reject or deny whatever is in our present moment awareness or in our life in general, we slow down or halt its evolution altogether.

Depression is a good example of how not allowing, accepting, experiencing, and investigating our feelings can keep us stuck in unresolved feelings. Depression feels like a dark cloud hanging over us, affecting our attitude toward life and our life force. We may think we're in touch with our feelings when we are depressed, but we're usually only in touch with our negative stories and the feelings those stories generate, not the feelings behind the depression.

Frequently, anger is beneath the depression, and beneath that are likely to be deep longings that have been repressed and not acted on. Fully experiencing and exploring the anger will bring any unacknowledged or frustrated drives or desires into awareness. When those who are depressed allow all of their feelings to be there and they spend some time investigating their feelings, what many discover is that they've been stopping themselves from following their heart for some reason, most often out of fear, often the fear of disapproval from others.

Depression and anger that isn't fully explored can lead to an unfulfilled life, to being stuck in a life that isn't the life you were meant to live, one that fits the unique person that you are. Anger and depression are potential wake-up calls, bringing attention to what needs to be seen for our further evolution. All of our stressful feelings have messages for us, and allowing, accepting, and investigating them is how we get to those messages.

One of the keys to being able to accept a stressful thought or feeling is realizing that accepting it doesn't mean you have to find a way to like that thought or feeling, which would be very difficult to do. Accepting a thought or feeling just means that you are willing to let it be there if it's there. If it's present, then let it be part of your present moment experience—because it is anyway. Allow it to be the way that it already is.

In some other moment, whatever is won't be. So you let whatever arises arise, and you let whatever leaves leave. Things, including thoughts and feelings, come out of the flow—the present moment—and then leave in their own time. This is the natural order of things. If we push a stressful feeling away or feed it, that will interfere with its natural coming and going.

I heard somewhere that an emotion has a lifespan of just a few minutes, and that's my experience as well, as long as we don't keep it alive with more thoughts and feelings. Letting a thought or feeling be there gives it the space to naturally move on and also makes space for investigating it if need be, since some thoughts and emotions that are recurring, persistent, and strong may need some investigation so that they aren't so convincing and "sticky."

Another key to being able to accept a stressful thought or feeling is, as already mentioned, realizing that it isn't *your* thought or feeling but our humanity's. Our thoughts don't mean anything; they're just thoughts that all human beings have. Since they aren't our personal thoughts, we don't have to feel bad for having them or for having the feelings caused by them. Not taking our stressful thoughts and feelings personally makes it easier to let them be there without trying to get rid of them or fix them, and without expressing them, which is one of the ways we try to get rid of or fix them.

This brings us to a third key to being able to accept a stressful thought or feeling, and that is compassion. Once we see that our thoughts aren't personal, we can have compassion for ourselves and all of humanity for the predicament we find ourselves in as human beings. We all have programming that leads to suffering, stress, and unhappiness, and overcoming this programming isn't easy. We are all doing the best we can with what we were given and with what we understand.

How fortunate it is that this same compassion, which is within each of us, can redeem us from suffering and heal our emotional wounds. We don't have to change or get rid of our stressful thoughts or feelings; we just have to bring compassion to them, and that compassion will transform and heal those aspects of ourselves that are out of alignment with our true nature. Do you have an inner complainer? An inner critic? An inner tyrant that pushes you to hurry up and be perfect? A scaredy-cat? Bring compassion to it and watch it melt away. These subpersonalities of the ego can't exist in the same space as compassion.

Acceptance, love, and compassion heal because these are qualities of our true nature. When we align with these qualities by evoking or finding them within us and expressing them to ourselves and others, we become our true self, and suffering ends. What we actually heal when we do this is the mistaken assumption that we are the separate, suffering self—that we are that complainer, critic, judge, perfectionist, scaredy-cat, or some other subpersonality. Acceptance, love, and compassion bring us back Home to our true self, back to the Noticer, where it's possible to recognize that we never were the self that suffers and is afraid of and defended against life and that the thoughts that caused that suffering were all lies.

Acceptance, love and compassion put our humanity into proper perspective, while enabling us to experience the greater, truer self: We are a spiritual being having a human experience, not the other way around. This realization, when it's not just intellectual, is transformative and freeing. What frees us is compassion for our humanness and the human condition. Without compassion, acceptance of our stressful thoughts and feelings and other people's would be much more difficult.

Compassion neutralizes our blame, anger, shame, hurt, resentment, lack of forgiveness, and fear by putting us in a new relationship to these feelings. That relationship is one of the loving and all-inclusive self to the fearful and limiting self. The true self feels compassion for the suffering self while recognizing that the suffering self is just ideas about oneself that seem true and real. The healing of these feelings comes from a shift in our identity from the false self to the true, compassionate self, which happens the instant we feel compassion.

It is this new relationship to ourselves that heals, one of kindness instead of anger toward and rejection of ourselves for being the petty, unkind, judgmental, and fearful self that we think of ourselves as. How freeing it is to realize that it's not our true nature but our false self that is petty, unkind, and afraid!

For the same reason, a relationship of a kind therapist to a client or the relationship of a kind parent or other adult to a child heals and brings out the best in us. Therapists, good parents, and even good friends heal our wounded heart and model the relationship we are meant to have with ourselves. They teach us what it feels like to love ourselves unconditionally, which is a tremendous gift. Unconditional love is what heals, and what makes unconditional love possible for ourselves and others is compassion for our humanity and the ability to see beyond our humanity to the divine in each of us.

So what in your life are you saying no to, are you not accepting? In other words, what are you resisting or what are you angry or upset about or wishing would be different? Take a moment and make a list of those things. List even minor things. Wanting these things to be different is what keeps you from being in the moment and from being happy. Your desire for these things to be different than the way they are is all that stands in the way of your happiness. And that desire is impotent. It doesn't change a thing; it only makes you unhappy.

If what you're saying no to is something you can change, does saying no to it help you change it? If resisting something helped us change it, then it would make sense to resist it. And if what you're saying no to is something you can't change, then what's it like to say no to it? Does saying no to it help you live with it? For instance, if you have a problem with your health, what's the effect of saying no to it—of being angry or upset about it or wishing it were different?

Unconsciously, we often believe that saying yes to, or accepting, something we don't like will perpetuate it, but that isn't so. Saying yes or no to something has nothing to do with whether something stays or goes, but it has a lot to do with how much we suffer over it while it's here. When you really see how ineffectual and stressful not accepting something you don't like is, that will help you live more easefully and peacefully with whatever is going on. We don't have to resist things. Resistance is the ego's automatic response to life. Once we become aware of the ego's resistance, we can become free of that resistance. Noticing resistance puts us outside of it and frees us from identification with the resistance and the suffering entailed in that.

Letting Go of Stressful Thoughts and Feelings

Often all we have to do to move beyond a stressful thought or feeling is just let go of it as soon as we become aware of it. It's much easier to let go of a thought, feeling, or desire as soon as you become aware of it than after you've fed it with your attention, since attention strengthens identification. Whatever we give our attention to gains power and becomes more difficult to let go of. With attention, a thought, desire, or feeling becomes more convincing, and more thoughts, desires, and feelings are added to it. Timing is key to the success of this strategy.

Letting go of a thought, desire, or feeling is not as difficult as some may think. We all know how to let go. We do it all the time. We have thousands of thoughts and many desires and feelings in a day that just pass by without contracting us. Because these thoughts pass by so easily, we don't feel like we're letting anything go. But we are. By not doing anything about them and allowing them to do what they naturally do — come and go — they naturally go, within seconds or minutes if we don't get involved with them. All we have to do is let them come and let them go in their own time. If we don't touch them, *they* let go of us.

Letting go is more a matter of *not* doing something than something that we do. The only thing we *do* is not give that thought another thought. Letting go is the natural result of not getting involved with a thought, desire, or feeling, of simply remaining an attentive witness to our experience. It is a matter of either not engaging in or disengaging our attention from stressful thoughts, desires, and feelings.

To do this, you first have to notice that you're thinking or feeling something that's causing you to contract, or that you're about to. This much awareness takes practice. We have to practice being mindful of, or witnessing, the coming and going of our internal and external experiences without getting involved with them in ways that produce stress. Meditation and mindfulness training teach us to do this, which is why these practices are so important to our well-being. More will be said about these practices in the next chapter.

When you first notice yourself getting pulled into a stressful thought or feeling, stop and take a deep breath, which will help you relax. Then just let everything be as it is, including the thought, desire, or feeling. Don't touch the thought, desire, or feeling; don't pick it up and run with it. And don't judge yourself for having it or go to battle with it or waste time wishing it weren't there. To counteract any tendency to resist or suppress it, try welcoming it. Smile and say to yourself, "Ah, you again, my friend. Thanks for sharing. Bye!"

Stressful thoughts and feelings are a natural part of the human experience. They don't belong to you personally, so you don't have to be ashamed of them or angry at them. Just let them be there. If you remain in a witnessing relationship to your thoughts and feelings, you will feel compassion and acceptance toward them and be able to remain nonattached to them instead of identified with and at the mercy of them.

Then from this place of compassionate acceptance, simply choose to let the thought, desire, or feeling go. Disengage your attention from the cause of stress and engage it in something neutral, such as some sensory experience you're having, or in something that helps you feel more peaceful and relaxed, such as a mantra, an affirmation, or an internal image of your dog or of a loved one smiling at you.

There's no need to be contracted and upset by stressful thoughts and feelings. It's in our power to notice, allow, accept, and let go of them, and put our attention on something else. We do these things as the Noticer, from the aspect of ourselves (the true self) that is aware of the thought, desire, or feeling and is capable of choosing whether or not to give it attention. The true self is what heals and frees us from the suffering of the human condition.

But how do you let go when it seems really impossible, when you're deeply identified with a thought, desire, or feeling? A related question is: How do you not believe a thought or desire when you believe it, when it seems really true or important? Isn't believing a thought or desire what makes letting go difficult?

The answer to both of these questions is that simply *intending* to let go or not believe a thought or desire has the power to release us from the grips of that thought or desire. This is truly mysterious. Releasing happens by simply having the intention to let go! All we have to do is let go as best we can in that situation. We're often able to let go of feelings this way as well, although we first have to experience them fully energetically without identifying with them (more about this later). As part of making such an intention, you might want to send out a prayer for help in letting go. Prayer is a way of giving more substance to our intentions.

What a marvelous gift this is that freedom depends only on intention and doesn't require philosophical or psychological acrobatics. The only trick is that the releasing might not happen the instant you make this intention, but repeatedly making this intention when a certain thought, desire, or feeling arises will eventually release you from it.

The beauty is that even when we have no such intention, we can only contract so long before we expand and feel good once again. When we are deeply contracted, it often seems like we'll stay that way forever. But consciousness, like the flow of life, never stays in one place. The natural order is for consciousness to expand and contract, just like the breath.

It might be helpful at this point to note that no matter how conscious we are and how much we may work at and intend to let go of a mood or a feeling, sometimes nothing seems to work and we are left with letting nature run its course. Like a storm, moods and feelings often take time before they let go and move on. All we can do at these times is be patient and compassionate with ourselves.

It's so important to be compassionate and gentle with yourself when you are contracted. Not being gentle with yourself will only keep you contracted longer. Getting identified with thoughts and feelings is part of being human, and as long as we are alive, we will probably never stop contracting. Nevertheless, the more awareness and understanding we bring to this process, the less we will suffer during it and the shorter and fewer the occasions will be.

The Sedona Method™, which is detailed in a book by that name by Hale Dwoskin, offers many inquiries and techniques to facilitate this process of letting go of thoughts and desires and releasing feelings. If you'd like to explore letting go more fully, I heartily recommend this book and the seminars offered that teach this method.

Investigating Stressful Thoughts and Feelings

We could just assume that any belief that contracts us isn't true and just let it go and be done with it. However, making that assumption often isn't enough to dis-identify with a belief and let it go. We might have to examine a particular belief more closely and come to that conclusion ourselves. Byron Katie, a renowned spiritual teacher, has developed a method to do this, which she calls "The Work." It investigates stressful thoughts with a series of four questions. I highly recommend her method for working with stressful thoughts. Here are her four questions:

- ❖ Is it true?

- ❖ Can you absolutely know that it's true?

- ❖ How do you react, what happens, when you believe that thought?

- ❖ Who would you be without the thought?

Byron Katie's first two questions point to what I've been pointing to: Are your stories, assumptions, conclusions, beliefs, opinions, judgments, fears, and even desires true? And can you absolutely know they are true? Just because we're convinced that a thought is true doesn't make it so. We have to look deeply into this illusion of thought and see if we really do know that what we're believing is true. When we question our stressful thoughts this way, we discover just how many unfounded, partially true, and false assumptions our egoic mind has.

As it turns out, there is very little that we know for certain, and yet we assume we know so much and that what we think we know is somehow more true than what someone else thinks he or she knows. This certainty of the mind is one reason relationships can be so difficult—we all assume we know things that we don't and that our way of thinking is right.

The third question—"How do you react, what happens, when you believe that thought?"—asks us to notice the effect that our stressful thoughts have on our body, on how we feel, and on our life. The purpose of this question is to help us see that we are hurting ourselves and possibly our relationships or others by believing our stressful thoughts. Once we see that our thoughts aren't true and that they hurt us and our relationships, the logical conclusion is to turn away from them. These questions are designed to help us break free from the egoic trance that we're all under as human beings. The trance is that we believe our thoughts even though they aren't true and even though they hurt us.

The fourth question—"Who would you be without that thought?"—points us to the fact that turning away from these thoughts not only saves us from hurting ourselves but makes it possible for us to be our best self and to be happy. Without our stressful thoughts, we would be kinder, more relaxed, more at peace, lighter emotionally, and more in tune with our innate wisdom and the natural flow of life.

These four questions are powerful tools for investigating our thoughts and easy enough to apply, but we have to be willing to stop before or in the middle of reacting as we usually do and take a moment to apply them. What is it that can make this choice to stop a moment and consider responding in a new way?

There's something here that is aware and realizes that the usual automatic and often unconscious reactions are detrimental and desires to change this. This is who you really are! It is right here, now, wanting to wake up and be more conscious, wanting to love and be happy and be at peace. Who you really are is waking up out of the egoic trance and using this information and your freedom of choice to do so.

Our conditioning has tremendous momentum, which compels us to act it out again and again. Without some tools, such as investigation and meditation, our conditioning often has its way with us. Will and commitment are needed to get beyond the momentum of this conditioning, to get at least somewhat outside its pull. Once we are, staying outside its pull becomes easier, and we begin to live more outside of the egoic trance than inside of it. But when we first begin to do spiritual practices such as meditation and investigation, a concerted effort and commitment is often necessary before our conditioning is no longer so compelling.

In the tradition I come from, which is called *nonduality*, investigation is called inquiry. The questions posed in this tradition are quite different from Byron Katie's, in that nondual inquiry points us beyond examining the content of a thought to who or what is having the thought.

Can you find a self who is having a thought? Or is thinking just happening? With this line of questioning, we begin to see what is meant by a false self, since what we discover is that there is no self who is thinking. The self that we think of as ourselves doesn't exist! We've thought it into existence! We think we are the thinker of our thoughts, but there is no thinker. There's no one to whom thinking is happening, only awareness of thoughts coming and going.

This question, "Who or what is having this thought?" moves us instantly out of the mind's virtual reality and the sense of being a separate somebody into reality and the great mystery of who or what is aware of thought. What is this Awareness that is aware of thought and everything else? Like a silent watcher and experiencer of life, it watches and allows the egoic mind to produce thoughts that appear to be *our* thoughts, but there is no self who is thinking these thoughts, only what seems to be a self. The false self is the self that seems to exist but doesn't actually exist. The false self is an illusion.

For many of our thoughts, nondual inquiry is enough to bring us out of the egoic trance and back into the present moment. When we catch ourselves lost in thought, we might simply ask: "Who or what is thinking these thoughts?" And instantly, we are outside of these thoughts, no longer identified as the thinker of them but as what is aware of them. However, some of our more persistent and emotionally-laden thoughts are likely to require an investigation of their content before we're able to stop believing them and move beyond our identification and fascination with them.

In addition to Byron Katie's four questions, I'd like to suggest another: "What are you afraid will happen if you stop believing that thought?" For example, if you stop believing that life is hard, you might be afraid that you won't work hard and therefore not survive. Or if you stop believing that you aren't loveable, you might actually have to experience being in a relationship and someone loving you, which could be scary and unfamiliar.

We often have a hidden agenda for believing what we believe and feeling the way we do, which keeps us from shedding our beliefs and letting go of our feelings. Underneath our more conscious beliefs are often numerous semi-conscious or unconscious beliefs that hold the conscious ones in place. Any such complex of beliefs is usually further strengthened and made more believable by a number of feelings.

For example, let's say your husband left you for another woman and you believe that he shouldn't have done this. This particular belief is likely to be connected to a number of others: "Marriage is sacred, and divorce is wrong. Men can't be trusted. He didn't love me. There's something wrong with me. Men always leave. Women are victims. Life is disappointing. I never get what I want." The list is potentially very long and so are the kinds of feelings these beliefs elicit: anger, jealousy, shame, envy, resentment, self-righteousness, sadness, guilt, desire for revenge, and hatred.

Every stressful belief is bound to have other stressful and untrue beliefs and feelings attached to it. Investigation involves investigating as many beliefs and feelings as possible within an emotional complex. So you would apply Byron Katie's four questions to the beliefs that you discover and work with each of the feelings that you uncover in a way that I'll describe shortly.

In this example, if you also ask the question: "What am I afraid will happen if I give up the belief that my husband shouldn't have left me?" what you're likely to discover is that by hanging on to this complex of beliefs, you get to hang on to the feelings. Why would you want to hang on to all those stressful feelings? Because they give you (your ego) a sense of identity. You get to be the wronged one, the betrayed one, the angry one, the self-righteous one, the one who's right, or some other identity. It doesn't matter to the ego that this is a negative and unhappy identity. The ego would rather feel right and self-righteous than be happy and free.

The ego has another agenda and that is to keep us tied to it. As long as we're stuck in feelings of blame, shame, resentment, anger, hatred, and so forth, we can't move on and be free of the pain of the experience of being cast aside. We'll be caught in our stories, feelings, and memories of the past, caught in the ego's virtual reality.

By feeding and perpetuating our stressful feelings with stories about how this shouldn't have happened, how awful he is, and how unlovable we are, we aren't being with our feelings in a way that allows us to take responsibility for them, heal them, and move on in our life. We're actually avoiding our feelings, although it may seem like we aren't, since we're so involved with them.

Furthermore, we're ignoring the complete picture, which would include other factors that contributed to the breakup, including our part in it. By asking, "Is it true?" of our beliefs, we stand a chance of seeing the situation from a broader, wiser, and more inclusive perspective, one that doesn't create unnecessary stressful feelings and continuing pain, and one that allows us to move on as gracefully as possible. Our beliefs, stories, feelings, and the identity we get from them keep us tied to them, stuck and unable to evolve and unable to close the door to the past and be in our life as it is showing up in the moment.

What prevents you from giving up your beliefs and your stories? If you gave them up and the stressful feelings that go with them, what would that mean and what would you have to feel? Wouldn't you actually have to feel that hurt instead of covering it over with anger or dressing it in victimhood or blame? If you felt that hurt, you would have the opportunity to get over that hurt, to see that even that is based on untrue beliefs. Stressful feelings are normal, but that doesn't mean we have to live with them forever and have them limit us and our happiness indefinitely. It's our choice to have this kind of a relationship with our feelings.

The ego isn't nefarious as much as it is primitive. As long as we are run by the ego, then our stressful beliefs and emotions rule our life. However, we are evolving as a species to a point where this emotional rollercoaster is no longer necessary. We don't have to be at the mercy of our stressful thoughts and feelings. We are evolving beyond them. Learning to investigate our stressful thoughts and feelings and be in a new relationship to them, which is one of not being identified with them while also being very accepting and intimate with them, is how we evolve as emotional beings and as human beings.

Investigating thoughts can happen in the moment they arise in the mind or at some later point when we have more time to explore, perhaps during meditation or some other quiet time. To get at what you are believing, you merely have to ask some questions: "What am I believing about this? What am I telling myself about this? What story am I telling? What spin am I giving this event? What meaning am I giving it?" These types of questions will help bring your beliefs to the surface.

This investigation is likely to be motivated by an unpleasant feeling and the desire to feel better. Feelings are our friends in this way. They point us to mistaken beliefs we're holding that may not be very conscious. By inquiring into feelings, we can uncover unconscious beliefs or stories we're telling ourselves that we weren't even aware of.

After asking, "What am I telling myself about this?" the next step is simply to listen. Be quiet and make space for insight to arise within you. Don't try to think of an answer; just allow an answer to come. For instance, in the previous example, if you're feeling hurt, ask yourself: "What story am I telling myself that's causing me to feel hurt?" Then listen quietly and patiently. You're likely to discover a number of different stories you're telling yourself that are making you feel bad. It might be helpful to write down what you discover so that you can go through the list later one at a time and ask, "Is it true? Do I absolutely know that this is true?" Then continue with the Byron Katie questions if you need to. If you have difficulty letting go of a particular belief or story, ask: "What am I afraid will happen if I let go of this belief or story?" Again, sit quietly and listen for the answers to come from within you.

By telling stories, our mind gives meaning to things. These stories create feelings. We can uncover the stories by asking, "What did I tell myself that made me feel this way?" For example, if you have a pain in your body and you start to suffer emotionally over it, what meaning did you give that pain? We often tell stories when we're sick or in pain that scare us and make us feel even worse. We tell ourselves we won't get better or that the pain or physical problem will ruin our life or kill us or that no one will love us. These stories add emotional pain to physical pain. Physical pain is much easier to accept and deal with without these stories.

So become very familiar with the mind's tendency to tell stories and try to catch the mind doing this as best you can before the stories turn into feelings. If you don't catch a story right away, then just investigate the feeling generated by the story to discover the story.

Exploration

> Examine any negative feelings that have come up during your day, such as anger, sadness, depression, shame, unworthiness, impatience, resentment, hatred, or jealousy. Do this examination in a quiet place where you won't be disturbed. In recalling these feelings, just be with them from a place of compassion, acceptance, and curiosity. Find out what you said to yourself and believed that caused you to feel that way. Negative feelings are a sign that you came to some mistaken conclusions. Those conclusions need to be discovered and seen to be false to loosen the power of those thoughts and feelings. Take plenty of time to do this. To uncover any fears around letting go of your conclusions or beliefs, ask: "What am I afraid will happen if I don't believe that anymore?"

Reframing Stressful Thoughts

The purpose of reframing is to arrive at a more complete and therefore truer story than the ego's story, which generally is limiting, negative, and only partially true and therefore causes suffering. This new story is inevitably a more positive and less stressful story and much closer to the truth and the perspective of the true self.

The perspective of the true self is inevitably more positive than the perspective of the ego because life is inherently good and moving toward greater love, strength, wisdom, growth, learning, creativity, and evolution on all levels. Life can be hard and challenging, but life's challenges develop, teach, shape, and evolve us. So the intent of life is good. It leads us, if we allow it to, to being better, wiser, and kinder people. That is its intent anyway.

Some may chafe at this characterization of life, especially those with more scientific minds. But I would argue that even if you don't believe or trust that life is good and meaningful, it's more functional to believe this than to believe the opposite, and that's reason enough to believe it! In other words, why not choose beliefs that help you live more happily and at peace with life and with others than beliefs that cause stress and interfere with being kind and happy?

Ultimately, we don't know for sure what life is about and what to believe about it. Nevertheless, our beliefs about it matter because our beliefs determine our experience of life and how we behave, including how we behave toward others. Being happy is largely a matter of jettisoning beliefs that sap our courage, strength, peace, and happiness and adopting ones that give us courage, strength, peace, and happiness. The beliefs that are helpful are inevitably positive beliefs, not negative ones. Even a positive fantasy is more functional than a negative fantasy, although positive fantasies are bound to let us down, while the greater truth about something, will not.

I'll give you a couple of examples of reframing from my own life. I could come up with many, many other examples — if I had a good memory! — and you probably can too. Many years ago, my second husband told me that he wanted a divorce so that he could be with another woman. I was devastated. Then it dawned on me that if this was good for his growth, it must be good for my growth too, because what's right for one part of the Whole must be right for all other parts of the Whole. I trusted that this was right for his growth, because he was so determined to take this course. He must have needed to do this for his own learning and evolution. This is what was happening, so it must be the right experience—for everyone involved—no matter how incomprehensible it might be to me.

That put the situation in an entirely new frame. Now I could see our divorce as an opportunity for me to begin a new life. Instead of feeling victimized, I looked forward to seeing where life would take me next. It must have something else in mind for me. What did life have in store for me now?

More recently, part way through writing this book, in fact just as I was ready to begin writing this section, tendinitis flared up once again in both my arms, forcing me to stop writing. Tendinitis had been a chronic issue for over a year, presenting me with a real challenge, since I love writing so much. I had already set a release date for this book, but now because of my arms, I didn't know when I'd be able to finish it, possibly not for many months beyond that date.

I had to confront the voices within me that said, "Hurry up and get it done. You have to get it done! What if I don't get it done? But I want to get it done!" I had to take a good look at these voices, these thoughts. Where they true? And what is it that wants to get something done even when I can't, even at the expense of my body? That can't be my true self.

I had to find a way to see this situation differently: What if getting the book done as fast as possible wasn't the best thing not only for me but for the book? What if not being able to work on the book was exactly the right experience? I asked myself, "How might this be the right experience? What is the gift in this? What positive effect is not being able to write having or what positive effect might it have on me and my life?"

When I realized that working on the book more slowly and taking more time with it than I had with my other books might even make the book better, then I was able to take a break and rest my arms. This shift in perspective enabled me to surrender to the reality that I couldn't write as I'd like to or as I had in the past. After some time, I could see that this was true — faster was not necessarily better. Things were getting added to the book that would have been passed over if I'd written it more quickly.

By reframing this experience (slower is better, at least for this project right now), I was able to see tendinitis as working for me and this book rather than against me. Even tendinitis was the right experience! I've since discovered many other gifts in having tendinitis. It forced me away from my computer and out of my head and back into real life, I gained a greater appreciation for the preciousness and importance of my health and body, I was humbled by experiencing my vulnerability in the face of something I could do little about, I learned to ask my husband and others for help with things, I began enjoying cooking again and paid more attention to my diet, I took more time to meditate and just be, and my relationship with Stillness became deeper (how appropriate!). And there are other gifts and possibly ones that I'm not even aware of, as there often are in the difficulties we face.

This is true of all our experiences — they are exactly right, whether we realize that or not. Seeing this truth about our experiences shifts us out of the ego's stressful perspective and the negative feelings created by that and aligns us with our true self's perspective, which brings peace and happiness to our heart. Reframing replaces the ego's perspective with the true self's, with a perspective that allows us to relax, feel good, love ourselves and others, and enjoy life once again. Reframing seeks to discover and highlight what is good about an experience rather than what we feel is bad about it.

By changing the way we look at something, reframing changes our experience of it. We no longer feel negative about it simply because we've changed the story we're telling about it. Reframing turns a tragedy or difficult time into a challenge and an opportunity for growth, which every difficulty is. Reframing looks for and focuses on the gift in an experience rather than on the negative, as our ego does.

Our default is to tell a negative story, which creates negative feelings, and these feelings are so unnecessary. We don't have to identify with our ego's negative stories. We don't have to feel bad. There's another possibility, and that is to replace a negative story with a positive one—one that contains more of the truth than the ego's narrow perspective.

Positive thoughts and feelings calm the body-mind and neutralize and protect against stress, while negative thoughts and feelings send our body into stress and fight or flight. When we bring positive thoughts and feelings to our experiences instead of negative thoughts and feelings, we enhance our health and happiness and consequently the health and happiness of those around us. Positive stories also improve our functioning and effectiveness, while negative ones do the opposite. When we're calm, we have access to our innate wisdom and the rational thought processes of the prefrontal cortex.

This is the power each of us has—to tell a positive story instead of a negative one. We can't change the past or the way life happens to be showing up in any one moment. We can't even stop our negative thoughts from showing up. But we can choose to think about our experiences in a way that causes us less stress and makes it easier for us to accept our experiences and be at peace with them. In fact, it behooves us to do so, or our health and happiness will suffer. It's your responsibility to find a way to be happy in the midst of difficulties. You are the only one who can make you happy by changing how you look at your experiences and the stories you tell about them.

To reframe an experience and move out of any negative feelings you are experiencing, simply become aware of what your mind is saying, recognize that what you're telling yourself is counterproductive (negativity serves no one except the ego), speak compassionately to yourself, and take some time to tap into and uncover a truer story, one that comes from a higher perspective—the perspective of your soul. How might the experience be serving your soul's growth? What might be the gifts in it? How might it be the right experience for now?

It may take some reflection to come up with an appropriate and true reframing, but this is important emotional and spiritual work that is well worth the time and effort and something that you'll get better at over time. Eventually, seeing from a broader and higher perspective will become natural and automatic.

A useful reframing technique is to view a difficult situation from a more zoomed-out perspective in relation to time. This technique provides a more complete perspective than the zoomed-in perspective of the ego. The ego sees difficulties through its narrow lens, through a particular story that is stuck in time and doesn't include a long-range view. When we find ourselves stuck in the ego's perspective, we can zoom out by asking: "How important will this be six months from now? A year from now? On my deathbed?"

The truth is that everything comes and goes, and fortunately this applies to our difficulties and our difficult feelings. The ego, in its tight focus, can't see that "this, too, shall pass." Reframing often involves putting whatever we're unhappy about into a larger frame, particularly a larger timeframe, which allows us to experience the problem from a more inclusive standpoint, one that lets us relax and be at peace with what is.

The signs that we have accessed the truth about something are a sense of peace and relaxation. Our mind and body get calm. On the other hand, when we're in the grips of the ego and its stressful thoughts, our mind and body are agitated, anxious, and tense. Noticing these different states within your body-mind will help you realize whether you are believing a lie or have found the truth about a situation.

This place of relaxation and acceptance is not only a place of truth but also a place where wisdom and solutions can be more easily accessed. Zooming out is not denying a problem but is actually a more functional place for dealing with our problems.

A variation on reframing by changing the timeframe is changing the timeframe of what we think needs to get done. So much of our stress is caused by believing that we need to get something done within a certain timeframe, as I did with writing this book. The timeframe we set for getting something done is often arbitrary and under our control, although it may not seem to be because we often really believe our own made-up timetable or someone else's. But that's how it is with the egoic mind—it makes up things and we believe it, unless we learn to question it. How do you create stress for yourself by declaring that you *have* to get something done now or within a certain time?

One of the ways the ego thrives and makes itself special is by making how much we get done overly important. Being overly busy gives us a sense of being somebody and often a sense of being somebody special. Being busy is the ego's mode, and we can easily get stuck in it, especially when those around us are also caught up in too much busy-ness.

I've noticed this sometimes in listening to others (and myself) describe all the things they have to do. They may be feeling exhausted and even martyred, but there's also often an unconscious sense of self-importance in their listing of what they have to do and what they've done: "Look how much I have to do and how busy I am." And because they're so busy and exhausted, others often are expected to make concessions for them. So this busy-ness can also become an excuse for being crabby or not taking time to relate.

The ego makes *doing* more important than *being* and more important than the quality of attention we give whatever we are doing. By pushing us to do more, the ego interferes with our quality of life rather than improving it. The ego limits our experience of life by keeping our attention on our to-do list and our story of how much we have to do instead of being in contact with the present moment and the real experience of life. If we actually made contact with real life, we would undoubtedly make choices more in alignment with our true self.

The ego has different values than our soul, our essence, and also often a different timetable. Essence will unfold our life and move us to accomplish whatever needs to be done within a certain timeframe, which is often a longer timeframe than the ego's, since the ego is all about speed and getting as much done as possible. To the ego, life is a race. What if speed and accomplishment aren't the highest values? What if trying to get so much done is actually interfering with your soul's agenda? Being overly busy may be serving the ego's agenda, but what about the soul's? What are you missing by being so busy and in such a hurry? Notice the fear and the striving to be okay and to live up to some ideal image that's behind the ego's agenda. Ultimately, that's what tends to run us ragged.

Taking on the ego's fear and perspective takes its toll on our happiness and health. The ego's way really isn't the way to live, even if most people operate that way. We live in an unhealthy society, and this will only change by each of us changing how we do things, which in many cases simply means slowing down our pace and the number of things we expect to accomplish in a day.

Here are some examples of reframing:

Negative story: "I can't believe I broke my leg! Now my summer is ruined."

Positive story: "I've always wanted to learn Spanish. Maybe this would be a good time to do that."

Negative story: "I can't believe I did that. I'm so stupid. I never do anything right."

Positive story: "Everyone makes mistakes. I won't make that mistake again."

Negative story: "It shouldn't have happened."

Positive story: "I'm lucky it wasn't worse."

Negative story: "I was counting on getting that job! What's going to happen to me now?"

Positive story: "There must be some other opportunity around the corner that fits better for me."

Negative story: "I can't stand him!"

Positive story: "He's doing the best he can."

Negative story: "I have to get this done."

Positive story: "It's not really that important."

Negative story: "What a bitch!"

Positive story: "She must really be stressed-out."

Here are some statements that can help reframe some of the negative thoughts that tend to run through our minds. You can probably come up with many more yourself:

I can't know this now.

It's not my business.

Everyone makes mistakes.

No problem.

It's not my problem.

It will get done.

No need to hurry.

It is what it is.

Everyone has challenges.

It doesn't matter.

It's not important.

All is well and unfolding as it needs to.

This too shall pass.

Love is more important than getting what I want.

There is quite a bit of support from neuroscience these days that shows that reframing can heal negative emotional states and memories. Neuroscience has shown that when two things are held in mind at the same time, they become linked and then re-stored in the unconscious together. So if a positive thought and positive feelings are brought to an unpleasant memory, those positive thoughts and feelings become part of the new memory. In this way, an unpleasant memory or negative story can be neutralized and the charge taken out of the feelings associated with it.

So when you find yourself stuck in unpleasant thoughts about the past, bring to mind someone who loves you or bring to mind a compassionate and loving presence, such as Jesus or the Buddha, or send love and compassion to yourself or anyone else involved in that memory, and that will help neutralize the negative memory.

Being with Stressful Feelings

In addition to investigating a particular feeling by asking yourself what you just said to yourself to create that feeling, you may need to take some time to be with a feeling to find out more about it and to calm it down. When the same types of feelings come up repeatedly, that means we need to spend some time with them.

Many of our feelings come from the hurt child that lives within us in our unconscious, and they come up whenever something triggers that emotional complex in the unconscious.

Such feelings are healed by being with them with acceptance and curiosity, just as a good and loving parent might be with a hurt child. Without such a relationship to these feelings, they'll continue to be triggered and are likely to be reinforced and even strengthened rather than healed, as we act them out in the usual dysfunctional ways.

Just as children need a patient, attentive, loving, and compassionate parent to soothe them when they are hurting, our feelings need us to listen to them patiently, compassionately, and lovingly. To heal and evolve, our feelings need us to just sit with them quietly, experience them, accept them, listen to them, and send love to them. This acceptance and receptivity toward feelings is often provided by a therapist or other healer or even a very good friend. But in many cases, we can provide this for ourselves.

In order to be with our feelings in a way that heals them, we first have to dis-identify with them. To dis-identify, we have to stop in the midst of feeling whatever we're feeling and notice that we're feeling something. Noticing that we're having a feeling and then making an intention to dis-identify with and heal it brings us into a new relationship with the feeling. We've taken a step back from the feeling, and now we're witnessing it. Now we have some choice about what to do next. We don't have to go back into identification and act out the feeling in the usual ways. We can relate to it from some distance.

It's important at this point that we relate to the feeling with compassion and not hostility or rejection. We bring compassion to the part of us that is experiencing this feeling, while staying in touch with the part that is able to witness the feeling and just be with it. Relating to the feeling from a place of a compassionate witness is what heals it. This compassionate witness is our true self, while the hurting self is the human self. We are compassionate toward our human self, while recognizing that it isn't who we really are.

As part of this process of dis-identification, it's helpful to keep stepping back into a broader awareness that includes not only the feeling but everything else that is present, because when we're identified with a feeling, that feeling looms large and blocks out the rest of reality. We can easily get sucked back into identification if we don't make a conscious effort at this point to move further into a more expanded awareness.

To help bring the rest of reality into focus and put the feeling in its proper perspective, we can ask ourselves: "Is there space around the feeling? How big is that space? Can I make that space even bigger? What is that space like? Is peace there? Is love there? Is compassion there? Can I be that space? What's it like to observe the feeling from the perspective of space? As space, what can I discover about this feeling? Can I, as space, give love and compassion to the feeling?"

When we do this, we discover that there's plenty of room in this wide-open spacious awareness for everything and every emotion, no matter how big a feeling may be. When we're able to identify with the spaciousness instead of with the feeling, the feeling is seen in perspective and seen for what it is—a feeling that comes and goes. It's just the conditioning we were given. We see that that feeling doesn't harm or affect who we really are: the spacious awareness in which the feeling is showing up. Because we see that having this feeling doesn't mean that there's something wrong with us, we can just let it be there, witness it, and get curious about it.

From that spaciousness, we can allow ourselves to fully have the experience of that emotion in our body without any story about it. We can let the feeling be as big as it is and as it needs to be. We can experience how it feels in the body, where it's felt in the body, what it has to say, and what it wants and needs. We can find out all about it. We don't need to change or fix the feeling in any way. We only need to be with it compassionately and let it be as it is.

When we simply sit with a feeling this way, any insight we need about the feeling will naturally arise, particularly insight into the beliefs that are behind the feeling. Sitting with a feeling this way is like listening to it. Our acceptance and receptivity open up the feeling, which relaxes, opens, and expresses itself, as it finally has our loving attention.

As the belief or beliefs behind a feeling are revealed, we accept these beliefs and have compassion for our humanness and the natural tendency to form mistaken beliefs. And we forgive ourselves for hurting ourselves by holding such beliefs. We may also need to forgive others, such as our parents, who taught us these mistaken beliefs. These individuals unconsciously and therefore innocently passed on their own misunderstandings and wounds. Forgiving ourselves and others helps us put these mistaken beliefs behind us.

When a belief behind a feeling is clearly seen, what often follows is a flood of tears. This release of feelings feels good, like a cleansing, and is often fairly short-lived. There is a cleanness about these tears, with no feeding them on the part of the mind. They suddenly come and just as suddenly end. Such tears are part of the healing and a sign that we have gotten to a core truth behind the feeling. Afterwards, as with a storm that has ended, the sun peeks through the clouds and we feel at peace. All is right with the world once again.

Here are two dialogues that illustrate this way of being with a feeling. These dialogues are between a therapist or compassionate guide and someone who is experiencing a feeling. Or they could represent an inner dialogue between your own compassionate self and the part of you that's experiencing a feeling:

Dialogue 1

Guide: What are you feeling?

Self: I'm feeling competitive, driven, like I want to get ahead and be ahead of everyone else. It feels mean and hard.

Guide: Stay with that feeling a moment and experience it fully.... Where do you experience it? How does that feeling feel in your body? How big is that feeling? What color is it?

Self: I feel it as a tightness in my throat and upper chest. It has sharp, knife-like edges, like ice that could cut you. It's like cold, gray ice. It's about a foot in diameter.

Guide: Now just let the feeling be and let it speak. What would that feeling say if it had a voice?

Self: It says: "I'm here to protect you. I'm the fight in you that keeps you independent and strong and not caring what others think of you. I'm the tough side. You need me to get along in this world. You need to pay attention to me or you won't be safe. If you don't listen to me, you won't ever succeed."

Guide: Just continue to experience that for a while and see if it has anything else to say or anything else it needs.

Self: It's afraid. It's small and feels unsafe and scared. It's little, like a child, not sharp and tough after all.

Guide: What is it afraid of?

Self: It's afraid of not being loved. If it isn't good enough, it won't be loved and it won't be taken care of. It won't survive. Life is hard. You have to struggle and fight to survive.

Guide: Is there space round this feeling, this contraction?

Self: Yes, there's space.

Guide: How big is the space? What is that space like—what are the qualities?

Self: The space surrounds it, like a halo. It's clear, simple, empty, plain. There's not much to say about it.

Guide: See if you can experience yourself as that space now. Can you?

Self: Yes, I think so.

Guide: Take a few moments and rest as that space.... As space, how do you experience the part of you that is contracted and scared?

Self: It's small, tight, dark, alone.

Guide: From your perspective as space, is there love and support for this scared part of yourself? What does the space itself feel for this part of yourself?

Self: It feels nurturing, compassionate, accepting and willing to just surround it until it feels better.

Guide: From space, give this contracted part of you whatever it needs. Allow the space's compassion, love, and softness to flow toward it and fill it up. That space is who you really are, and that contracted place is just visiting you for a while. Welcome that tightness, let it be there, and just stay in the compassionate space awhile, giving love to the scared part of yourself. And invite that part of yourself to reveal anything else that needs to be understood about it. Just stay in this place of compassion and receptivity until it feels complete.

Dialogue 2

Guide: What are you feeling?

Self: I'm angry at my husband for being sick all the time. We never do anything. We never go out. All we ever talk about is his health.

Guide: Where and how do you experience this anger in your body?

Self: I feel a tightness in my gut and a sadness in my throat, like I want to yell or cry. It feels heavy and gray. I'm sick of him being sick!

Guide: Just stay with that experience in your body awhile and let yourself feel it fully on an energetic level. Let me know anything else you experience or if it changes.

Self: Nothing's changed. It still feels as strong.

Guide: Good. Just stay with it…. Of course you feel this way. It's natural that a part of you is angry and sad when your husband is sick so often. Anyone would feel this way. Can you feel compassion for the part of you that feels this way?

Self: Yes. It feels bad to feel hard and closed off from him and from being happy. This part of me is not happy.

Guide: Just keep sitting with this part of you, be there for it, and keep sending it love and compassion. You don't have to do anything else but just sit with it. Just let it be as it is and be there for it in case it needs anything. You don't have to fix it or have it change in any way. Just let it be…. What's it like for you now to do that, to give it your attention and to give it space to just be?

Self: It feels good to feel compassionate. I feel softer and more open toward myself and my husband. I guess it's normal to feel this way and I can just accept that about myself. It feels like there's more here now than just feeling angry and sad, like those feelings are just part of what I'm experiencing, because I'm also experiencing this softness too.

Guide: How about asking this part of you that's angry and sad if it needs anything. Is there something you can do that would help it to feel better?

Self: It says: "I need to get out more. I need to get away and do some different things. I need to play and have fun."

Guide: Is that something you can do?

Self: Yes! Just because he's sick I don't have to stay home all the time. I can still have fun.

Guide: Would you be willing now to send love and compassion to your husband, who is going through a difficult time too. Just call him up in your imagination and allow yourself to feel the love and compassion you have for him. And then wish him well: "May he be happy. May he be at peace. May he be well."

Self: Yes, it would feel good to do that.

Our thoughts and feelings don't have to result in stress once we change our relationship to them and stop seeing them as *ours* and accept them as part of the human experience, as something that every human being experiences and will always experience. We can't rid ourselves of our thoughts and feelings; we can only learn to relate to them in a new way, one that creates less stress.

Once we realize that our thoughts and feelings are simply the experience of our body-mind, of our humanness, we can then also experience the compassion — and love — that our true self has for this experience of being human. The human self is beloved by the Divine. When we can contact the Divine within us, we can move much more gracefully through life as this human self.

CHAPTER 4

Present Moment Awareness

Living a stressful life and being stressed-out is a habit, one that may be difficult to see a way out of. But there is a way, and that is to learn to become more present, more in your body and senses and in whatever experience you are having *now*.

When we are present, we are not only able to notice, accept, and detach from our own egoic mind, but also from other people's and the stress that their judgments and opinions so often cause. We're also able to be in relationship to other environmental stressors, such as noise and heat or cold, in a way that can minimize their impact on us.

Presence

The experience of the present moment is an experience of Presence. It is called Presence simply because it's what we experience when we are fully present. Although Presence is too mysterious, rich, and profound to be captured by words, we have many words for it, including Stillness, Silence, Ultimate Reality, the Now, Essence, the Sacred, Wholeness, the Mystery, the Divine, "the peace that passeth all understanding," Unity, Oneness, Love, Truth, and Awareness. These are all attempts to describe the ineffable experience of being in touch with who we really are.

We use words such as *stillness, silence, peace,* and *love* to describe Presence not only because we become still, silent, peaceful, and loving when we're in Presence, but also because when we become still, silent, peaceful, or loving, we drop into Presence. Thus, many of the words that describe Presence are both a description of and a prescription for experiencing it.

Presence is a sense of connectedness with everything, a sense of unity and belongingness, a feeling of being home, being held in a mysterious, unimaginable, and benevolent universe, at one with life and with the Divine that is behind all life. When you are in Presence, your boundaries soften and expand to include everything you're experiencing. Your sense of *me* is replaced by a spacious beingness that feels complete, holy (whole-y), content, and fully alive. Presence is a state of complete contentment and happiness. You feel like there is no other place you'd rather be than where you are and nothing you'd rather be doing than what you're doing. Presence is the fulfillment we are all searching for.

Each of us carries the experience of Presence within us, because it *is* us. Life gives every one of us brief experiences of it even daily. Then one fine day, the experience of Presence becomes a realization of an ongoing reality, as we recognize that Presence is the true and only reality, the Truth, not just a passing euphoria or spiritual experience. We see that Presence is the ever-present reality, our very own divine self, made manifest in this beautiful world through us.

When you have a deep experience of Presence, you recognize that it's the experience that mystics have described throughout time. Many have pointed to this great mystery at the core of our being, but until we have eyes to see, we don't see it. Once we do, we are forever changed by it, as we can never experience life the same. Our eyes have been opened, and they can't be closed to the Truth again, although we may temporarily lose sight of it.

Presence is both simple and ordinary, and most extraordinary. It is our happiness and fulfillment as human beings, the culmination of our journey as a human being: to discover that, in fact, we are one with that which created us. We are and always have been divine.

Being Present

Everyone knows how to be present because everyone knows how to pay attention. Being present simply means giving our full attention to whatever is happening here and now rather than being lost in our thoughts. Being present is being aware of reality, noticing what's being experienced by our body and senses. We can also be present to our more subtle, internal experiences, such as intuitions, urges, feelings, and thoughts.

When we're present to our thoughts, we are witnessing them rather than identifying with them. We notice a thought and then move on to noticing what else is showing up in the moment. When we are present, we notice everything in our experience. Our awareness moves around, taking in the entirety of what is being experienced, without getting stuck in the mind's virtual reality.

The alternative to being present is being identified with the voice in our head. We all know what that's like. When that happens, we could have eaten an entire piece of cake or walked two blocks without noticing anything about the experience. We were lost in the virtual reality of our thoughts. We were still able to function—we still ate and walked—but we weren't present to the experience that our body was having. It's as if we didn't have that experience. Many of us live most of our lives in this state of non-contact with reality. We are asleep to the aliveness and richness of reality, cut off from our essence, our soul, a prisoner to our egoic mind.

Everyone moves in and out of being present throughout the day. Our attention moves back and forth between our world of thought and real life as it is unfolding. We bounce back and forth between being present and being lost in our inner world. Our thoughts are part of reality, but they have the unique ability to draw us into a virtual reality that then colors and at times covers over the experience of the present moment. Like no other aspect of reality, our thoughts draw us out of reality into an alternative reality. This alternative reality is the cause of suffering, as it is the source of our negative feelings. It is the source of the false self.

Being focused mentally isn't always a place of suffering, however. Being absorbed in mental tasks, such as reading, planning, watching a movie, or playing a video game, is generally enjoyable unless the egoic mind is wanting to do something else, complaining, or being judgmental. Whether we suffer or not as a result of being involved in the mind depends on whether we're involved with the egoic mind or simply using our mind to work or play.

As fun as it is to use our mind, if these activities aren't balanced by contact with reality, we'll feel drained and ungrounded. In order to feel good, balanced, and whole, we need contact with reality, which requires being in our body and senses. When we shift from being mentally focused for a long time to being externally focused and in contact with reality, we experience an aliveness, juiciness, and beauty that can't be matched by virtual reality, not even by our pleasant experiences of virtual reality.

Being present renews and energizes us. This is why meditation is so refreshing and particularly necessary in our world, where we spend so much time plugged in to either our egoic mind or our technological devices. Many of us don't fully appreciate the richness of reality because we go from involvement with the ego's virtual reality to the virtual reality of our iPads, TV, and movies, with very little time spent smelling actual roses.

Being involved in the virtual reality created by our thoughts about ourselves is especially exhausting. Many of us are worn out, not so much because of what we do, but because of all the emotions that are generated by listening to our egoic mind while we're doing what we do. We may think that listening to our mind helps us accomplish things, but more often, it drains us, particularly if those thoughts result in negative feelings.

We need contact with reality. To be mentally and emotionally healthy and even to be sharp intellectually, we need to move out of our egoic mind and the emotions it creates and into reality. Not spending enough time in reality causes us to lose our balance and perspective. We become narrowly focused, zoomed in, on our to-do list or some desire or problem, as defined by the mind, and the rest of reality falls into the background. We need the rest of reality to keep us in balance, to remind us that our thoughts are a very small part of reality, and not a very real part.

The real problem is that the ego thinks that being present is boring and without value. We're programmed to believe the opposite of what's true! How amazing that is. And how will we ever discover the truth if we keep allowing the egoic mind to pull us out of the present moment? We'll never find out how to really live life if we continue to listen to our thoughts. There's another way to live, and that is, very simply, to pay attention to your present moment experience. Notice your thoughts as they arise in the mind, but give your attention to what's actually happening.

Throughout your day, you are present to some extent. But to what extent and for how long? This is key. Are you present to life just enough to not have an accident, for instance, while continuing your mental monologue? How long do you dip into the present moment before you're back in your thoughts?

At times, we do dive into our present moment experience, and those are happy times. The more you are engaged with the present moment, the happier you'll be. Here are some examples of ordinary moments throughout the day when you might find yourself being present and happy:

You suddenly see an eagle flying overhead, and you gasp and feel yourself expand with delight.

Your dog rolls over for you to rub her tummy, and you feel so much love for her. You are taken by her sweetness and innocence.

You see the first flower of spring, and your heart leaps for joy.

You sink into a warm bath, and all of your cares melt away.

Your favorite song comes on, and you're overtaken by happiness.

You gaze into the fireplace on a cold winter night and feel that everything is perfect.

You're walking through the woods and filled with awe at the beauty of the light shining through the trees.

You're lying in a hammock, looking up at the sky and feeling expansive.

You tuck your child in bed and feel tremendous love and gratitude for the gift that life is.

You dive into a lake and feel at one with the water as it slides over your body.

You see two children walking hand-in-hand and feel the love that they are sharing.

You take a bite of your favorite food, and you feel transported.

You put some dance music on and lose yourself in it.

Your lover tells you how much you mean to him, and your heart fills with joy.

You tell your lover how much he means to you, and your heart fills with joy.

What moments would you add to this list? Moments such as these can be extended by choosing to stay in them longer. While even a brief experience of being present is wonderful and refreshing, if you're able to stay present longer, that experience will deepen, strengthen, and become more natural. Being present turns into an experience of Presence when you stay present long enough.

By staying present a little longer, you'll become more familiar with Presence, and you won't want to go back to your old way of being. The ego doesn't want you to taste Presence deeply, because once you do, the Truth can no longer be hidden from you.

To stay in Presence longer, notice the sensations of opening, expansion, awe, joy, love, and peace and give them some attention. Stay with these subtle sensations a while. Whatever we focus our attention on becomes magnified. Really feel what awe, joy, love, peace, and expansion feel like. Explore them with your awareness. What a mystery! Relish these sensations, knowing that they are the experience of your true self.

This is what it feels like to be alive as your true self. This is how we are meant to experience life. Any moment can be an experience of peace and contentment if peace and contentment are what you give your attention to.

Becoming Present

If loving something means giving it our attention (and it does), then most of us are in love with our thoughts. The irony is that this lover doesn't love us back but, instead, gives us a lot of negative messages and poor advice. In short, this lover makes us unhappy. What can explain our devotion to such a poor lover? This is a strange situation we find ourselves in, like so many love affairs: We can't live with the egoic mind and we can't seem to live without it. But we can!

You can live without the egoic mind, but you won't discover that unless you're courageous enough to give it a try. Like giving up a bad lover for no lover, giving up the egoic mind can be scary. Give it up for what? For the present moment. You fall in love with the here and now, which is all you really have and have ever had. Nothing in your mind actually exists.

Of course, to the mind, turning our attention to the present moment seems unsafe, not to mention boring. These two things — fear and boredom — keep us from experiencing the richness of life without the egoic mind. We believe the mind when it tells us that it's not safe to leave it behind and that there's nothing for us in being present — and there isn't, for the ego, that is.

There are a number of keys to becoming present, which we will explore next:

- ❖ Being in the body and senses,

- ❖ Being willing to not know,

❖ Accepting life,

❖ Being grateful, and

❖ Giving love.

Being in the Body and Senses

To fall in love with the present moment, we first have to *experience* the present moment. After all, how can we love something that we don't even know? Many of us spend so much time in our head that we aren't even aware of what we're experiencing through our body and senses. We barely touch in to our experience before we quickly return to our world of thought, our virtual reality.

Most of us spend most of our time partially in our head and partially in our body, or moving so quickly between the two that these are not two distinct experiences. Rather than experiencing reality purely, we have only one foot in reality and the other in virtual reality.

Practices like yoga and Tai Chi are meant to bring us out of our head and into our body. When we shift our attention to the experience that our body is having, we naturally move out of our head, because we can't be fully in our body and in our head at the same time. Moving out of our head naturally brings us into the present moment, because there is nowhere else to be! When we leave our virtual reality, all that's left to experience is reality.

Reality is an experience of being fully in our body and senses. We also have an intellect that processes that reality. But essentially, the experience of reality, of being in the moment, is a sensory one: We are hearing, feeling, seeing, tasting, and smelling life. We are also sensing the more subtle aspects of life that are part of our internal experience, such as energetic sensations, intuitions, urges, motivation, and inspiration. Thoughts and feelings are also part of our internal experience, which if given attention, create our virtual reality.

What is it that is having this simple sensory experience of life? That is the real you, and it's the only you that actually exists. Who you really are is what is experiencing life through your body-mind, although you aren't a thing but more of a verb. You aren't an experiencer as much as the experience of experiencing. What the mind brings to this is a sense of being someone, of feeling like someone who is experiencing life. And so the false self is born. But actually you are the mysterious experiencing of life that is happening through the vehicle of the body-mind.

All you can know of who you really are is your experiencing of life through your body-mind. So to become more present and to experience Presence, you have to pay attention to the experience that this being that you are is having through your body-mind. The egoic mind and other programming that give us the sense of being someone keep us at a distance from this raw, stripped-down experience of life. But this experience *is* life, and it is all we really have, while the experience of being someone is an illusion, an imagination. It's a useful imagination when we need to function in society, but it's still an illusion.

The false self is like a ghost that's taken possession of us. It's having its way with us and causing us a lot of suffering. We need to realign with who we really are. Then we will use our conditioned identities only when we need them, without being run by them. We'll move in and out of these identities as needed in order to function and interact with others, while knowing that we are not these identities. This is freedom. This is where everyone's spiritual evolution is headed. Eventually, we all uncover who we really are and learn to live as that.

The way this transformation comes about is by becoming more aware of our living experience, without the influence of the egoic mind:

❖ *What is it like to be alive, to see, to hear, to feel, to smell, to taste, to think, to be?*

❖ *Who would you be without your thoughts about yourself?*

❖ *How would you move?*

❖ *What would you choose?*

❖ *How would you interact with others?*

Stripped of our thoughts about ourselves, we would all be kinder, wiser, happier, and more at peace. We would glide through life, in the flow, without a sense of having a problem or lacking anything. Everyone has moments like this. The key to having more of them is being really present to what you're experiencing through your body and senses.

To get into your body and senses, just pay close attention to what you're experiencing right *now*. Pay attention to *everything*, not just one aspect of your experience. Notice how your awareness moves around, taking in the various aspects of this present moment. Notice the ingredients that make up this unique moment: the sensations, what you see, what you feel, the thoughts, the sounds, and your internal experience. Every moment is a unique blend of these ingredients—a special soup. What's your soup like right now?

This soup is always changing, which makes life interesting. There's always something new to pay attention to. Even when little is going on externally, our inner landscape of intuitions, urges, inspiration, dreams, imaginations, longings, sensations of expansion and contraction, feelings, and thoughts is constantly shifting. One moment, our soul is soaring; in another, we are contracted over some thought.

Thoughts and feelings aren't a problem when we're present to them in the same way that we are present to every other internal and external experience. Thoughts and feelings are just part of what the being that you are is experiencing. They come and go like every other experience if you don't get upset about them or feed them with your attention. Just stay present to them and allow them to exist, and then allow them to disappear. Everything is coming and going in this one timeless present moment.

When you are busy during your day, you can anchor yourself in the present moment by periodically reminding yourself to pay attention to the sensations in your body. Or you could stop a moment and just listen to the sounds in your environment and the silence in between the sounds. Paying attention to all of your senses at once or singling out one sense, such as hearing, works like a meditation to bring you into the present moment. If you do this for a few minutes, you'll experience your being relaxing, and you'll enjoy what you're doing more.

Another anchoring device is to notice the aliveness that is present in your hands. Aliveness is the felt sense of who we are. It is how your being is experienced by the body-mind. Aliveness is experienced as a very subtle, energetic tingling. It can be experienced in any part of our body, but it's easiest to experience in the hands.

Take a moment right now to see if you can experience the aliveness in your hands. To feel the aliveness, you have to stop what you're doing and thinking and pay attention to your hands. Stopping and paying close attention to anything, as long as it's not the voice in your head, will immediately bring you into reality. Can you feel the aliveness in your hands? How about in your arms or other parts of your body? That aliveness is the force that enlivens you.

If you're feeling stressed-out during your day, it may be helpful to do some inquiry in addition to anchoring yourself in the present moment:

1. Stop whatever you are doing and become curious about your present moment experience. Ask yourself: "What am I experiencing right now internally and externally?" Give yourself a moment to experience the range of sensations, thoughts, and emotions that are present.

2. Spend some time with the energy of the contraction caused by the stress you're feeling. We usually run away from our internal experience when it's unpleasant. But let yourself be with the contraction for a moment. Experience what it's like to be contracted and feel the way you feel.

3. Then do some inquiry to see if you can discover the source of the stress and contraction. Is there something you just said to yourself or that you've been telling yourself that's making you feel stressed-out? Are these thoughts true? Do you need these thoughts? What if you didn't listen to these thoughts but relaxed and took your time doing whatever you are doing? If that would be difficult, what beliefs keep you from relaxing and enjoying what you're doing?

When you begin doing something again, really let yourself experience that activity with all your senses. Anything can be enjoyable if you're present to it and let the experience be whatever it is. Even sitting in a doctor's office can be pleasant.

There are always sights and sounds to enjoy wherever we are. How can you make the best of the experience you are having? Usually just having the experience you are having as fully as you can without the egoic mind's spin is enough to enjoy life.

Being Willing to Not Know

To fall in love with the present moment, we have to fall in love with not knowing, because the present moment is an adventure in not knowing. We have to be willing to get lost in the moment and let life take us from one moment to the next without knowing where it's taking us. Life is doing that anyway, whether we like it or not!

The truth is that we have never actually known what the next moment holds, even though the mind usually pretends to know. Based on the past, the mind assumes to know what's going to happen or it imagines a desired future. This tendency to make up the future or pretend to know what's going to happen is what egos do to feel safe. It's an attempt at some control in a world where little is, in fact, in our control.

The ego pretends that reality is different than it is. Then when reality doesn't match the ego's desires and assumptions, it's disappointed or angry. These feelings result in stress. But that doesn't prevent the ego from continuing to pretend that it knows and continuing to create an imaginary future. Our minds are just programmed to do that.

The trouble with believing the mind's version of reality is that it takes us out of reality, which is a very pleasurable experience. Being in the moment is highly pleasurable because being fully in our body and senses is highly pleasurable. When we spend enough time in the present moment for the depth of sensual pleasure to register, we are rewarded, and this encourages us to spend more time there.

Although the ego seeks sensual pleasure, it's usually lost in thought or doing two things at once while engaging in that pleasure, thereby diluting the sensual experience. Ironically, the ego seeks pleasure, while limiting the experience of pleasure by keeping us in our head in the midst of whatever sensual experience we're having.

What makes being in the moment difficult has nothing to do with the present moment, because the present moment has everything we've been looking for. What makes it difficult to be in the moment is that the mind constantly pulls us out of the moment. Thoughts are extremely seductive, and we are programmed to be seduced by our thoughts.

Our programming causes us to believe that our thoughts are more important and juicier than anything going on in the moment and that the present moment is bland and boring, when quite the opposite is true. Thoughts are actually poor imitations of reality. Like cardboard pictures of a piece of cake, our thoughts entice us but don't deliver anything real.

How could the ego, or why would it, give us anything truly satisfying when its purpose is to produce discontentment? The discontentment it creates keeps us involved with it, as it attempts to solve the problems and satisfy the dis-ease that it has caused. The ego thinks up problems and then offers solutions. But its solutions, like its problems, are made up. They are artificial and don't arise naturally from the present moment, from the flow of life.

Have you noticed how life solves problems? Answers, solutions, arise all of a sudden out of nowhere when you need them, but not necessarily exactly when you want them. Who knows when that will be? That's how the present moment works.

It delivers answers and solutions when the time is right. We just don't know when that will be. That's why to fall in love with the present moment, you have to fall in love with not knowing.

What's so bad about not knowing? Nothing, really, if you trust life. The ego doesn't trust life, so its solution to not knowing and to the distrust engendered by not knowing is to pretend or try to know something. But when you trust that life is good, you don't need to know. For instance, when you trust your husband (or wife) to pay the bills, do you need to know about it? No. Trust precludes knowing. Not needing to know allows you to drop out of your egoic mind into the moment. Once you are in the moment, life is a sensual and joyous adventure.

When you are in the moment, you experience life as the being that you are experiences life—and it's having a wonderful time! It's in awe of the life that it has created and is participating in. It's excited to see what will happen next and how life will unfold: Who will show up? What will that person say? What will I say? What will that person do? What will happen after that? What an adventure this is.

The way to experience life as an adventure instead of something to be afraid of is to fall in love with not knowing what's going to happen next. That's what we love about movies and novels, isn't it? We love to wonder, and we long to find out what's going to happen. What will that character do? And then what?

The Divine is having a ball creating and living within its creations in each of us. What an amazing gift life is! This is the truth that the ego doesn't want you to see, because if you do, you'll realize that you don't need the egoic mind anymore. Then it will fall into the background and become irrelevant.

Accepting Life

Acceptance and other qualities of our true nature, such as gratitude and love, are keys to becoming present, because expressing these qualities aligns us with our true nature. Even just being *willing* to accept, be grateful, or love can align us with our true nature. Just the intention can take us there!

That's really good news, because accepting life can be a real challenge. We are programmed to want things to be different than they are. Like a two year-old, our ego says no just to say no and express its autonomy. Just because the mind is able to imagine how life could be better, it claims that it *should* be. But life doesn't work that way. Desiring doesn't make it so, and our imagination has only a minimal impact on reality.

Accepting something doesn't mean you have to like it, however. It only means that you're willing to have it be the way it is, even though you may not like it. You're willing to surrender to the reality of what's showing up in your life right now. After all, what's the alternative? Acceptance means not fighting or arguing with reality.

If something is the way it is, then the only reasonable thing to do is to accept it, since it's already too late to change it. Certainly, we can take steps to change whatever we don't like. However, the voice in our head doesn't help us do that. What the voice in our head says doesn't affect what's actually happening. It only affects how we feel about what's happening. The egoic mind just complains about and judges whatever's happening. This isn't constructive, doesn't change a thing, and only makes us miserable. The ego's alternative to accepting reality is being upset about it! That isn't a very good alternative. Once we see this, then acceptance becomes much easier.

For example, the thought that you wanted your spouse to do something doesn't change the fact that he didn't do it or make it more likely that he will do it. That desire is irrelevant; it doesn't change reality. It only makes you feel disappointed. The voice in our head is what causes us to suffer—not what's happening. What's happening is just happening, and the voice makes us unhappy about it.

To stay in the present moment, the attitude is, "Ah this... and this... and this too." Being present is an attitude of noticing what is, accepting it, and then responding naturally to it rather than to how we think life could or should be or how we'd like it to be. For instance, if you chip a tooth, you call the dentist. You don't need to turn the chipped tooth into a drama by lamenting, "Why do these things always happen to me! Now I'll have to pay for this on top of everything else," and go on to list all the reasons why you don't like the fact that you chipped your tooth. We do this, don't we? We build a case for how awful life is and, in particular, how awful life is for *me*.

We are not in control of what happens. The ego is angry about that. But what good does that do? The ego tends to take life personally, as if life should cater to its wishes and demands. When life doesn't, the ego feels angry and victimized. The ego is childish and egocentric.

Life isn't about making our egos happy. It has its own purpose for being, which is mysterious. When we accept that life is the way it is, we can enjoy the mysteriousness of life and the surprising turns it takes. Acceptance allows us to go with the flow and tap into that which is within us that is wise and capable of being happy under any circumstances.

I was surprised to discover this innate acceptance when my beloved dog had a tumor biopsied and we were waiting for the results. I wondered: "Is this how life is going to play out now? Is it time for him to leave us? What would that be like?" I felt curious and surrendered to the possibility of his death, recognizing that we aren't in control of what happens and also trusting that whatever happens is the right experience for everyone.

Life is much wiser than I am. It knows what's best for the Whole. I don't. Such trust allows us to relax and let life play the cards that it's going to play. It's going to play them anyway. It's crazy to be upset about it. If you are upset, that's a sign that you've identified with the part of yourself that doesn't trust life: the ego.

This doesn't mean that I won't cry when my dog does die, which thankfully won't be due to that tumor, since it turned out to be benign. But it means that I won't suffer unnecessarily because I believed that he shouldn't die. I know that the reality is that everything eventually dies.

When we accept reality as it is, we drop into the present moment, where we can enjoy everything that's happening: the blessings and the challenges. From that place of acceptance, it's all interesting. It's all good. This that we are loves a challenge! Can you find the place within you that loves a challenge, that doesn't categorize everything as either good or bad?

The freedom to not be tossed to and fro by our mind and emotions is what we all ultimately want. What we really want is freedom from the ego, freedom from suffering. We want to be free from negativity, free to love, free to be at peace. Accepting what life deals us allows us to experience that freedom.

Being Grateful

Gratitude is another key to becoming present, because gratitude, like acceptance, is also a quality of our true nature. Our being is grateful for the gift that life is. When you aren't feeling grateful, thinking of something you are grateful for will align you with your true nature. From there, you can discover the possibility of being grateful even for what you don't like.

No matter what's going on, there's always something to be grateful for. In fact, there's always a lot to be grateful for. Our being is even grateful for challenges because they provide us with an opportunity to grow and learn. Although it might be difficult to be grateful for an experience like an illness or losing a loved one, we can always be grateful for the courage, strength, patience, compassion, wisdom, and any number of other qualities that are developed as a result of such an experience. These qualities may not be apparent immediately, but it is a rare individual that doesn't become stronger and more compassionate as a result of difficulties.

To shift from non-gratitude to gratitude, all we need to do is stop focusing on the mind's complaints and start focusing on what's showing up in life that we *do* like. Doing that drops us into the stillness, peace, and joy of our heart.

Life and everything on this planet is a gift to us. It was all given to us for us. When we realize how much is given — the sky, earth, trees, water, sunshine, every living thing, and the body and senses to enjoy them — we can't help but be grateful. Isn't it amazing how we're provided with roads, food, the internet, someone to cut our hair and fix our computer, trucks to pick up our trash and maintain our city, information from around the world to enrich and entertain us, dogs to keep us company and make us smile, flowers to decorate our home and open our heart, plants to take in our carbon dioxide and give us oxygen, rain to water the flowers and food, gravity to hold us on the earth, an imagination and a mind to create new things, beauty everywhere we look, and most of all, the capacity to love. How infinitely more things could be added to this list!

Everything that happens is support for your life and every other living thing. Isn't it a miracle that what each of us offers the world provides us with this support? There may be times when you feel that this support is inadequate or lacking. But you are still here, so something is supporting you in being here even in those times. Everyone is contributing and everyone is receiving. We're all working together, breathing in the same air and breathing out the same air, like a single organism.

We're all moved to contribute, and we're moved by something very mysterious. How is it possible for this immensely complex existence that we are part of to function and support us? Isn't this such a miracle! What good fortune it is to be born into a world that provides for us. Some would argue that it doesn't do this very well. But truly, isn't it amazing that it does it to the extent that it does! There's so much to be grateful for.

Something behind life moves each of us to contribute as we do. We have enough people doing the things that need to be done to make it all work. How does that happen? We didn't all decide to be doctors, for instance. That would be too many doctors! Some of us had to be patients, anyway. Each of us is playing our role. What is behind our choosing to do what we do? Life is a great mystery.

When I can see that others are playing their role perfectly (and as a bonus, they're doing it with their own style and unique personality), then I can relax and just let it happen as it is happening and feel grateful for life unfolding as it is. Something much wiser than we are is making it all happen through us. How interesting! I think I will just enjoy the unfolding of the show in front of me. Maybe I'll jump up and do something too. Who knows? It's fun not knowing, especially when you realize that we are in good hands.

Even those who cause difficulty and trouble have a place in this mystery. They serve a role too. It may be hard to see how they're contributing, but at the very least they contribute to our growth and evolution by challenging us. And sometimes we are the one causing trouble! I'll let the troublemakers be as they are too, since they are as they are. I'll let them be part of this drama on earth, since they already are. I might be moved to do something in response to them or not. We'll see. It might be someone else's role to respond instead.

We all have a part to play, and we just need to play that part. We can hardly *not* play our part. So I'll let life be as it is and let it move me as it does. And I'll revel in this great mystery and bring as much consciousness, gratitude, and joy to it as I can. To see the truth about life—that we are part of one Consciousness that is creating it all—is to be happy and at peace. From that place, it's easy to be grateful.

Practice

During your day, tune in to the excitement that your being has in being alive. Notice this, however subtle. The more you notice it, the less subtle it becomes. The experience of being in the moment is potentially intensely pleasurable, in part because of this excitement that the being that you are feels in simply being alive. Can you experience your being rejoicing in life, even just a sliver? Focusing on that sliver of excitement will magnify it.

Giving Love

Expressing love is one way to instantly return to our natural state, because our true nature is love. Why do we love to be in love? Because it brings us the peace we have always wanted. When we love, we are content at last. We can finally rest and be happy. Ironically, the ego takes this truth and seeks love from the outside. The ego seeks to *be* loved, while the secret to experiencing love is to *give* love. As usual, the ego has it backwards.

Because love is our true nature, we are never apart from it, although we aren't always aware of the love at our core. But when we express this love, we experience it. As if by magic, love suddenly appears, seemingly out of nowhere. But it was always there. It just needed to be expressed.

We feel this love as it's flowing out of us to someone or something. When we're in love with someone, we make the mistake of thinking that the love we're feeling is coming from the other person. We think that person is giving us love, when all that person is doing is waking up the love that's inherently ours. Fortunately, we don't need others to wake up this love. We can wake it up ourselves by simply choosing to express it.

However, although love is our natural state, giving love isn't so natural because our default state is the egoic state of consciousness, and the ego's mantra is, "What's in it for me?" If we're able to turn this focus on *me* around to focusing on reality and giving love to whatever we are experiencing, our state of consciousness will be transformed. We will relax, our energy will open and expand, and we'll begin to enjoy life. This very simple act of shifting our attention from *me* to reality is the difference between hell and heaven, stress and Stillness.

Expressing love can be practiced, and the more it's practiced, the more natural and rewarding loving becomes. The act of sending love to ourselves or others is what Buddhists call the practice of loving kindness. The great news is that it doesn't matter what you send love to, because the result is the same: You feel good!

You can send love to anything: a tree, a car, a stranger, a bee, traffic noise, the rain, a scraped knee, a parking lot, anger, or a judgment. And if you're having difficulty with someone, send love to that person. You can do this by imagining love flowing to that person, by thinking of something you appreciate about that person, or by saying something kind to that person.

A good place to start is to send love to yourself, especially when you're stressed-out or being hard on yourself. Think of what you appreciate about yourself or say something kind to yourself. Or imagine that someone who appreciates you is being loving toward you. You could also imagine a wise, loving being, such as the Buddha, Jesus, or Mother Mary, emanating love and compassion toward you. Imagining your dog giving love to you also works! Our pets are often the easiest ones to send love to and receive love from because they're nonjudgmental.

To send love, all you have to do is make that intention and then take a moment to find and then feel the love that's already there in your heart. If you can't find a feeling of love immediately, try thinking of someone or something that's easy for you to love, like your pet or your child. Or remember a moment when you felt full of love, such as when your child was born. Or spend a moment taking in something beautiful. Notice how your heart opens when you stay with the experience of beauty. Beauty brings us Home. Then move on to finding the love in your heart for what may be more difficult to love.

Give your attention to any bit of love that you're able to experience and hold your attention there long enough for that bit of love to grow into a more encompassing experience of love. Then notice the sense of relaxation and peace that comes with loving. Love is its own reward.

One of love's outward expressions is a smile. If you're feeling stressed-out or unhappy, smiling will help you shift to a more relaxed state. Smiling sends a message to the brain that all is well and fight or flight is unnecessary. Did you know that even just imagining yourself smiling or seeing someone else smile makes your brain light up as if you were smiling? My mother's advice to put on a happy face was wiser than I thought. In the case of smiling, faking it will help you "make it."

The practice of giving love may take a little time to develop. But with practice, calling love forth becomes easier and more automatic. Love, instead of stress, can become the state you live in most of the time. We are here to learn to love. There's no more important lesson.

Spiritual Practices

The purpose of spiritual practices is to bring us into Stillness, into that "peace that passeth all understanding." Spiritual practices help us to become more present and to express Presence in our daily life. Three important spiritual practices are prayer, breathing practices, and meditation.

Prayer

I'm assuming that, since you are reading this, you're interested in transforming yourself. I'm guessing that you'd like to be happier, healthier, more peaceful, and more loving. These are our deepest desires and birthright as human beings.

Prayer is an excellent tool for transformation, because in prayer, we both acknowledge the need for change and express our willingness to change and grow. For example, in the Serenity Prayer, "God grant me the serenity to accept the things I cannot change, courage to change the things I can, and wisdom to know the difference," we acknowledge that we need and want acceptance, courage, and wisdom. Making such a statement takes insight, humility, and sincerity, which are key to transformation.

What follows is a general prayer for transformation that you can modify to suit your needs. Add whatever else you'd like to, to this prayer, including specifically what you want healed, what you'd like insight about, what you need acceptance for, what you want to let go of or forgive, and so on.

I am willing and ready to receive help in…

Seeing whatever needs to be seen,

Doing whatever needs to be done,

Healing whatever needs to be healed,

Understanding whatever needs to be understood,

Accepting whatever needs to be accepted,

Letting go of whatever needs letting go of,

Forgiving whatever needs to be forgiven,

Growing in whatever ways I need to grow.

When we declare such intentions, we connect with the loving forces that are guiding us and all of life. These forces celebrate our desire to be happier, to grow, and to be more loving and at peace. When we pray, spiritual forces come forward to do what they can to help us move in our intended direction.

These forces are ever-present and eager to support us, but because they respect our free will, we have to ask for their help. If we're attached to our negative thoughts and feelings and making no effort to be free of them, then spiritual forces let us have this experience until we're ready for peace and happiness. They allow us to be victimized by our egoic mind as long as we're willing to be victimized.

One of the ways that spiritual forces know we're ready for a new relationship to life is through a statement of our readiness, such as a prayer. It is a very powerful prayer, indeed, that declares our desire for freedom from ego-generated suffering. Such a prayer signals a point in our evolution when we are ready to wake up from the illusion that we are who our thoughts tell us we are.

Prayers help us feel connected to something greater than ourselves. Feeling connected in this way brings peace, and it is the truth: We are connected to and part of everything. Moreover, what we are connected to is benevolent! This understanding is so important in being able to relax and let life be as it is. We are safe. Life is good. We are love. And we are eternal. The more we know this, the easier it is to do what we need to do to be in the moment, such as to be in our body and senses, to relish the adventure of not knowing, to accept life, to be grateful, and to be loving.

Even if you don't believe that spiritual forces exist to support you, prayer has a psychological value. A sincere prayer summons and fortifies our will. It strengthens our resolve to be transformed, to move beyond our limiting conditioning and old habits. Prayer is a way of declaring to ourselves and, more importantly, to our unconscious mind that we intend to change. In a sense, we are giving a heads-up to our unconscious mind that, going forward, it's not business as usual.

Rituals and initiations perform a similar function. Prayer, rituals, and initiations are ways of demarcating the old from the new, of starting fresh, of wiping the slate clean. This is important and often necessary psychologically to move into a new way of being. We first have to see ourselves differently in order to be different, and rituals, initiations, and prayer can help us do that.

The power of prayer comes, in part, from how easy it is to do. It's so easy to do that you can do it many times a day, whenever you're feeling beleaguered by the mind. We need something this easy and at our fingertips to help us overcome our relentless negative programming. A simple prayer like "Help me to accept this" or "May I be more present" might be all you need to shift out of negative thoughts. Here are a few other suggestions for prayers that you might say in the course of your day:

Help me to (or May I) know what to do now.

Help me to know what to say now.

Help me to see the Divine in everyone.

Help me to see the good in X.

Help me to be more loving to X.

Help me to quiet my mind.

Help me to be happy.

Help me to let go.

Help me to be patient.

Making a prayerful statement stops the egoic mind in its tracks and replaces its words with words that help you step outside the mind. Prayer is a way of snatching the reins from the ego. Prayer can help you become more established in the moment and less at the mercy of your negative programming.

I saw a documentary the other day about Wavy Gravy, who is a peace activist and clown dating back to the 60s, a real American saint, in my opinion. The film showed him praying at an altar, which he does each morning. His prayer was: "May I be the best Wavy Gravy I can be today."

I love this prayer because all we can do and all we have to do is be the character that we came here to play to the best of our ability. We can't be someone else nor can we be perfect, according to some ideal. We can only do our best to be the character we were intended to be. Some days, or moments, our ego has a hold of this character. On other days, or moments, our true self shines through, with love, wisdom, and a twinkle in the eye.

Breathing Practices

Breathing practices are part of many spiritual traditions, because breath connects us with our spiritual self. Breath makes it possible to be alive and conscious. It is what enlivens the body at birth and what is absent at death. Breath is evidence of the mysterious, mystical force, or spirit, that moves us and experiences life through our body-mind. What are we if we are not this very force that animates the body-mind? We are what moves the body-mind. Everything is moved by this same force. Everything is alive with the same spirit.

Our breath is connected to consciousness in another important way: Changing how we are breathing changes our consciousness. Some go so far as to suggest that it doesn't matter how we alter our breathing, because altering it in any way will shift our consciousness. The most common ways of altering the breath are:

❖ Breathing faster,

❖ Breathing slower,

❖ Breathing deeper,

❖ Holding the breath, or

❖ Breathing through alternate nostrils.

So changing our state of consciousness is as easy as changing how we're breathing for even just a few minutes. We can also change our consciousness by focusing on our breath or by counting our breaths. What a profound discovery it is that doing something as easy as this can transform our state from stress and angst to peace and relaxation.

Because of this ability to relax us and calm our mind, breathing techniques are a perfect prelude to meditation. Many people complain that they can't meditate because their mind is too busy. Spending just ten minutes doing some breathing practices before meditating is the cure for a busy mind and will make meditation much easier and deeper.

There is another advantage to breathing practices: They can strengthen our connection to the unconscious, allowing unconscious material to surface and be healed. Doing breathing practices regularly can also help us access dreams, insights, intuitions, and creativity.

Breath also has a profound effect on our physiology. Both focusing on the breath and breathing more deeply and slowly balance the sympathetic and parasympathetic nervous systems. Dr. Andrew Weil in *Breathing: The Master Key to Self Healing* (an audiobook by Sounds True) asserts that most people in our stressful world have an overly active sympathetic nervous system, which mediates the fight or flight response, and an underactive parasympathetic nervous system. He explains that when this imbalance continues for a long time, it can result in certain physical disorders, including high blood pressure. By strengthening the parasympathetic through breathing techniques and meditation, we can regain our equanimity and health. Practicing certain breathing techniques has also been shown to reduce anxiety and insomnia and improve circulation and digestion.

The most basic breathing technique, taught by many spiritual traditions, is simply to pay attention to your breath, without holding it or trying to change it in any way. Just notice your breath as it naturally cycles in and out. As you do this, notice the sensations related to breathing: how the air feels as it enters and leaves your nose, the temperature and softness of the air, any sound it may make, how it feels on your upper palate and throat, how it feels in your lungs, and how it moves your abdomen in and out. When your attention wanders, which it naturally will, gently bring it back to your breath.

Meditation on the breath is the most fundamental meditation taught. It's simple, tried, and true. As a variation of this basic meditation, on the in-breath, you might say to yourself, "May all beings be happy" (or "May I be happy"), and on the out-breath you might say, "May all beings be at peace" (or "May I be at peace"). Those particular prayers come from the Buddhist tradition, but you can use any phrase or mantra that appeals to you.

Another variation of meditating on your breath is to count your breaths. You can count each cycle of inhalation and exhalation as one, or you can count "one" on the inhalation and "two" on the exhalation. When you get up to ten, begin counting again. If your mind wanders, just begin at number one again. This breathing technique is easy, and it's fun to see if you can get to ten. With practice, you'll be able to do several rounds without losing your focus.

A couple of things will make these meditations on your breath more powerful. One is to make each inhalation and exhalation deeper and slower than usual, without straining yourself. The other is to try to make the inhalation and exhalation the same length. We tend to spend less time exhaling than inhaling, which leaves air in our lungs and limits our inhalation and therefore the overall depth of our breathing. To even out your breaths, try counting to four on both the inhalation and exhalation. For a deeper breath, count to ten or to whatever number is comfortable.

Another tip for making the most of meditating on your breath is to breathe from your diaphragm. This means breathing in a way that expands your diaphragm, or upper abdomen, rather than your chest, which is why this is also called abdominal breathing. With diaphragmatic breathing, your chest and shoulders should not move; only your diaphragm moves in and out slightly. This is a healthier way of breathing than from the chest, because breathing from the diaphragm expands the lungs more fully, allowing a greater intake of oxygen. Diaphragmatic breathing is how we're meant to breathe. Breathing that moves the chest only rather than the diaphragm is considered shallow breathing and is associated with repressed emotions and stress.

The beauty of breathing practices is that many of them can be done anytime without anyone even knowing that you're doing them. So if you're feeling hurried and stressed-out while waiting in line at the supermarket or bank, focus on your breath for those few moments. Doing that will be good for your health and well-being and good for everyone around you. Whenever you're feeling hurried, anxious, stressed-out, or annoyed, you can make it a habit to focus on your breath for just a few minutes. Those are particularly good times to add the Buddhist prayer or some variation of it: "May all beings be happy."

Because breathing practices prevent a thought from taking root and blossoming into a feeling or mood, they can be especially helpful when you wake up in the middle of the night and can't get back to sleep. Doing these practices then will cause you either to fall back to sleep or have a quiet mind when you finally do get up.

You only need to set aside a few minutes a few times a day for your breathing practices. Good times for doing breathing practices are when you wake up, before you go to sleep, before you meditate, or before meals and, of course, whenever you feel nervous, anxious, or upset. It's best to sit with your spine straight in a quiet place where you won't be disturbed, just as you would for meditation. There is no more important stress-relieving technique than working with the breath. It's important enough to write an entire book about, but it's too simple to fill a book, although I'm sure someone has!

Meditation

The purpose of meditation is to still the mind. Although we can't make the mind become still through force of will, meditation naturally results in a quieter and more peaceful body-mind and moves us into a place where, even if the mind still chatters on, we aren't involved with it. Meditation accomplishes this by focusing the mind on something: the breath, a mantra, sounds, music, sensations, a mental image (as in a guided meditation), a picture of a saint, a yantra or mandala, or the movement of the body (as in yoga or Tai Chi).

When the mind is still, it's much easier to experience who we really are, which is the purpose of meditation. The purpose is not to have a spiritual experience. If having a spiritual experience is your goal, you might become discouraged with meditation if you don't have the desired experience, which would be a shame. Spiritual experiences come and go, but the experience of our true nature is always here and available whenever we turn our attention to it. Meditation familiarizes us with our true nature, which enables us to live more as that, and that is much more valuable than any spiritual experience.

Once the mind is stilled sufficiently or there's enough dis-identification with it to experience your true nature, then rather than continuing to focus on whatever you were focusing on, another possibility is to continue with a less focused meditation. Stay with the experience of Stillness and with the experience of whatever else you are experiencing. Simply notice whatever you are noticing and experience whatever you're experiencing through your senses or internally, without getting involved in any thoughts about what you're noticing, sensing, and experiencing and without trying to change anything about your experience. If you find yourself involved in thinking, then as with a more focused meditation, gently bring yourself back to noticing, sensing, and experiencing whatever you are experiencing.

The more focused meditations, such as focusing on the breath, are a good preparation for this less focused type of meditation, which is an experience of just being. In this less focused type of meditation, you're taking time to simply experience, sense, and be. This is what the being that you are is actually doing all the time. We align with our being by experiencing, sensing, and noticing, without getting involved in the mental commentary that tends to draw us into the ego's world. Instead of experiencing life through our ego and its mental constructs, as we're used to doing, we experience, sense, and notice life as our being does.

For those who would like to learn more about meditation, particularly about the more focused type, in the Appendix I've included an excerpt from one of my other books about how to meditate. There are many wonderful books dedicated to this most important spiritual practice, such as Sarah McLean's *Soul-Centered: Transform Your Life in 8 Weeks with Meditation*. Meditation is so simple that you don't really need to study it to do it. However, reading about meditation can inspire you to begin a practice of meditation, help you to stick with it, and give you the confidence that you're meditating correctly.

I encourage you to make meditation part of your daily life. People often brush meditation off, saying it's too difficult or that it doesn't work for them. But even when meditation seems difficult and you feel like you're getting nowhere, it's still helpful. Meditation is one of those things that we do for our long-term well-being, like eating healthy food. Although you may not notice the effects of meditating immediately, any time that you spend doing it is always beneficial, whether it seems so or not.

Having said that, I'd like to offer some facts about the benefits of meditation and mindfulness, which might motivate you to begin a practice or to meditate more regularly and for longer periods of time. For millennia, the East has recognized the power of meditation and mindfulness. It's time for the West to embrace these practices as well. Our world needs them now.

Mindfulness is a type of meditation from the Buddhist tradition that trains us to be aware of our moment-to-moment experience. It teaches us to directly experience whatever we're experiencing without the coloration of the egoic mind's judgments, fears, beliefs, preferences, and stories. It trains us to be present to reality, to life as it actually is, rather than lost in the past, the future, and other mental constructs.

Mindfulness is a practice we can do not only on our meditation cushion but throughout our day. Being mindful in our daily life is being aware of and present to whatever is showing up. Mindfulness cultivates a way of being that makes us happier, healthier, more effective, more in touch with our spiritual nature, and more peaceful and loving.

Mindfulness meditation has been researched extensively in recent years, particularly by Jon Kabat-Zinn, Ph.D., who has been a strong proponent of it in the West. Kabat-Zinn's research demonstrated that just eight weeks of mindfulness training was enough to reduce anxiety and depression and teach people to be more present. Mindfulness has also been shown to be useful for hypertension, chronic pain, trauma, and addictions and for improving eating and sleep patterns and strengthening the immune system.

According to Daniel J. Siegal, M.D. in his book *The Mindful Brain,* the practice of mindfulness results in a change in the structure of our brain, specifically in the prefrontal cortex. This change in our brain, in turn, makes it possible for us to more easily be in a mindful relationship to life on a more ongoing basis. In other words, by changing our brain, meditation changes how we are in life. Dr. Siegal lists a number of effects that a practice of mindfulness or meditation can have as a result of strengthening the prefrontal cortex:

- ❖ Greater ability to pause before reacting to stimuli (improved impulse control),

- ❖ Greater empathy and compassion toward others,

- ❖ Greater insight, self-understanding, and intuition,

- ❖ Greater sense of well-being and peace,

- ❖ Greater emotional balance, and

- ❖ Greater ability to regulate and override fear.

Tara Brach, Ph.D., clinical psychologist and the author of *Radical Acceptance,* explains that because mindfulness and other meditation practices activate the prefrontal cortex, which correlates to positive emotions, and deactivate the limbic system, which correlates to fear, a practice of meditation helps us maintain a positive attitude toward life and to be less fearful. This is a much more functional way of being—and it feels better too.

Furthermore, as part of the limbic system, we are programmed to resist pain, including emotional pain. However, emotions are healed, not by resisting them, but by welcoming, accepting, and being curious about them. Meditation supports emotional healing by developing the part of our brain that can override the limbic programming that resists emotional pain. In this way, meditation can help us master our emotions rather than be ruled by them.

Brach also explains that noting or labeling an emotion, as is often done in mindfulness practice, as well as writing or talking about our emotions activates the prefrontal cortex and calms the limbic system. This change in our brain makes it easier to dis-identify from a thought or feeling, which results in a peaceful state. For example noticing and stating, "Fear is here" evokes a completely different state than "I'm afraid." Identification with fear ("*I'm* afraid") amplifies the fear, while noticing fear doesn't. Noticing our emotions puts us outside of them, at a distance from them, where we can objectively see the truth about them—that they're generated by the egoic mind.

The long-term effect of both mindfulness and meditation is that these practices help us recognize the egoic state of consciousness and train us to move out of that state and live more from another, more positive state, which I've been calling Stillness. This shift in our state of consciousness is essentially what spiritual growth and our evolution as human beings is all about.

Bridges to Presence

We often look to our mind to change our state of consciousness. We try to fix our state by thinking about it as if it's a problem to be solved by the mind. We ask, "What do I need to think or understand or do to feel better?" And we listen to the mind's advice, when the egoic mind is the problem, not the solution. What we're looking for can only be found by dropping out of the busy mind that created the stress and unhappiness in the first place.

What follows is a list of things that you can do to drop out of the mind. It summarizes some of the suggestions already mentioned. These suggestions are bridges that can take you from the egoic mind to Presence, even in the midst of a busy day. Most take very little time. Try them out and see which ones work best for you and what you most enjoy doing. If you do them often enough, they'll become habitual and automatic. When you notice yourself feeling stressed-out, do one or more of the following:

❖ Stop whatever you're doing and take a break,

❖ Slow down enough to really experience what you're doing,

❖ Pay attention to your breath for a few minutes,

❖ Take a few slow, deep breaths,

❖ Meditate or sit quietly for a few minutes,

❖ Notice what is aware. What is it that is conscious and aware?

❖ Pay attention to the sensations in your body,

❖ Notice the aliveness that is present in your hands, arms, and entire body,

❖ Pay attention to the sounds in your environment and the silence in between the sounds,

❖ Pay attention to something of beauty in your environment and notice how beauty opens your heart,

❖ Smile,

❖ Affirm a truth, such as "All is well and unfolding as it needs to, Let it be, It is what it is, Whatever will be will be, It doesn't matter, This too shall pass, It's all good,"

❖ Send love to someone or something: trees, cars, people, etc.,

❖ Think of a person or pet that you love,

❖ Imagine that someone who appreciates you is giving love and appreciation to you. Or imagine a wise, loving being, such as the Buddha, Jesus, or Mother Mary, emanating love and compassion toward you,

❖ Note what you appreciate about yourself or someone you're having difficulty with (to counteract self-criticism or judgment),

❖ Say something kind to yourself or to someone else,

❖ Forgive others for their unpleasant behavior and wish them well. Forgive yourself for your imperfections, bad behavior, or not being able to do everything you think you should be able to do,

❖ Bring to mind what you are grateful for,

❖ Pray for help: "May I be at peace. May all beings be at peace,"

❖ Give yourself a few moments to experience the energy of the contraction caused by stress and whatever you are feeling. Let everything be and naturally unwind,

❖ Inquire, "What thought, belief, or story is causing me stress or keeping me from being present right now?"

❖ Notice what you're thinking and question whether it's true,

❖ Notice the pushy, "hurry-up!" mental voice and don't follow it,

❖ Remind yourself to let everything to be as it is.

CHAPTER 5

Changing Your Lifestyle

Making Time for Stillness

In our culture, being busy is the norm. Doing and being productive is our god, a value we've elevated above many others. Because it's valued so highly, being busy makes us feel special, important, and successful. So it's not surprising that so many people seem to be addicted to being busy. They may even actually be addicted to the adrenaline rush that often comes with being under pressure and moving at a fast pace.

If we aren't as busy as everyone else, it can be hard to feel good about ourselves. When I couldn't work and was resigned to doing very little, I assumed that this period of disability was intended for my growth, which I'm sure it was. But why does every moment need be seen as purposeful? Isn't this just another version of the ego's need to always be accomplishing something in order to feel okay? Why is just *being* considered a waste of time, while doing almost anything is considered worthwhile? Whose assessment is this? Isn't this just the ego's point of view?

Not being busy can feel like a problem for another reason: It often stirs up our fears, since doing is the ego's way of feeling safe and in control. When we are identified with the ego, doing becomes a way of life, since not doing or just being seems dangerous to the ego. Won't we perish if we stop doing things? The ego thinks so.

Survival seems dependent on doing, which to some extent it is. But the ego doesn't acknowledge the survival value and importance to our well-being of resting, contemplation, and connecting with others and with our deepest self. Of course, the ego doesn't really want us to connect with our true self. All of this busy-ness keeps us living the ego's superficial life rather than a more meaningful life, one guided by our heart.

Here are some questions to ponder:

❖ *What do you get from being overly busy? Does it make you feel special? Important? Safe? In control? Powerful?*

❖ *What identity would you have to give up if you slowed down? The winner? The martyr? The achiever? The perfect one?*

❖ *What negative identity might you give yourself if you slowed down? Lazy? Unsuccessful? A Loser?*

❖ *What beliefs or fears keep you from slowing down? What are you afraid would happen if you slowed down? Are you afraid that if you are peaceful and relaxed you won't survive or achieve what you'd like to achieve?*

❖ *What would you have to feel and experience if you slowed down that you don't want to feel or experience?*

❖ *Is there something in your life you'd like to change that you aren't changing? Instead of doing something about that, are you compensating and trying to feel good by acquiring things and achieving status?*

Being relaxed and peaceful is actually a very functional state, not a less functional one. Being overly busy and stressed-out is exhausting and distances us from our creativity and deeper wisdom, which help us perform better. Relaxation is a highly effective state, the most effective state, and periods of relaxation are necessary to function at our best.

Some people are afraid that if they are relaxed and peaceful, they'll become lazy. They imagine that if they stop being so busy, they'll stop doing altogether. But relaxation and laziness are not the same thing at all, although the ego would have us believe that. "Lazy" is a judgmental label that the ego uses to keep us in line and on track to do its bidding. It's a way of shaming us into more activity.

"Lazy" is what we call ourselves or what others call us when we don't want to do something. But not wanting to do something often just means:

❖ It isn't aligned with our heart,

❖ It's not the right time to do it (it's not coming out of the flow),

❖ We don't see it as necessary, or

❖ It isn't important or of value to us.

If we're feeling lazy or depressed, that is, if we're lacking motivation, it's probably because we haven't connected with our heart and discovered what we're innately motivated to do. Our heart naturally moves us to do what's meaningful for us as well as necessary for our survival. However, our beliefs and other conditioning can interfere with this natural movement.

We might also feel lazy or depressed simply because we're so tired out from being so busy doing things that aren't fulfilling.

Taking time to relax is necessary to maintain a balanced, healthy, and happy life. Relaxing is not a waste of time nor a lesser state than being active, but a sacred state in which we are both renewed and in contact with the deepest truth of our existence. Relaxing is *not* doing nothing.

If we learn to relax by taking time to regularly relax, the bonus is that we'll be more relaxed in everything we do. We'll bring this relaxation to our work, our relationships, and our world, which so desperately need this. Imagine what a different world this would be if everyone felt relaxed instead of stressed-out.

When you do just let yourself be, when that is appropriate, doesn't it feel wonderful and right? Doesn't it rejuvenate you and help you face your day freshly and with greater clarity and wisdom? So how can that be a waste of time?

It's important to catch the ego's subtle judgments so that they don't completely shape our life. If we assume that resting, just being, and meditating are a waste of time or luxuries that we can't afford, then of course we won't make room for them, and our life will remain out of balance.

Look what happens when we let the ego's perspective shape our lives: The result is stressed-out, exhausted, and unhappy people and a society that spends its free time consuming and pursuing pleasures and addictions to assuage an empty heart. It isn't healthy for us or for our children to have every minute scheduled. The lifestyle that the ego creates doesn't leave time for creativity, contemplation, spirituality, relationships, renewal, just being, and also being present to whatever we *are* doing.

The heart and soul can be put back into society and into our lives by periodically allowing ourselves to just *be*, preferably each day. Time just being is not only not a waste of time, it's likely to be the most valuable time you spend each day, as it can determine how you'll approach your day, what attitude you'll bring to it, and what you'll choose to do. Just being puts us in touch with our internal guidance system, which is necessary to live a happy and fulfilled life.

Unless we make an effort to include meditation and just being into each day, most people don't make time for these things. In our modern lives, there's no natural or easy stopping point, when we can say, "Okay, I'm done for the day." Even the end of the workday is not the end of work for many people, thanks to technology. It's certainly not the end of their to-do list. There's always more to do, because the to-do list is constantly being replenished.

Life keeps bringing us more to do, more email, and more information to process. We'll always have things that we feel we need to do. If we wait for our to-do list to empty or for an easy stopping place, we'll never make time to just be. We'll never "have time" to do anything but what's on our to-do list.

When do we draw the line and say, "That's enough. Now it's time to stop and rest"? Unfortunately, many of us never do. We don't even see how it's possible. We claim, "I don't have time" without questioning this assertion. Making time for one more thing, like meditating or resting, seems impossible. Will you ever have time to step off the hamster wheel? When will you finally choose to and find out what happens?

What is the result of never having time to stop, rest, just be, contemplate, and connect within? For many, the result is a breakdown of their body. They keep going until their body gets sick and can't go anymore. Is that when you'll finally let yourself stop? I don't mean to sound accusatory. I count myself among those who couldn't stop working until their body gave out. Illness is a time when many discover that they do, in fact, have time to stop. Because they have to, they adjust their life and others adjust theirs to accommodate their illness.

When we willingly choose to slow down or stop, the same thing happens: Life adjusts to this choice, and you discover that you *can* slow down and you *do* have time to stop. Then that new pace becomes your norm. When we stop for a bit or slow down, life goes on—and it feels better. But you won't discover this unless you give it a try.

Of course there's time. There is always time. Time is a mental construct. It's an idea. And the idea that you don't have time is just a belief, not a reality. For the most part, you create your to-do list and you execute it. You can just as easily change your to-do list and slow down the execution of it. Don't let the ego, the inner time tyrant, push you around.

The way to begin changing the habit of not taking time to stop, rest, and just be is to put resting, just being, and meditating on your to-do list every day! Just as you take time each day to get dressed, feed yourself, and sleep, you can take time each day to check in within and just be.

Just being and spending time going within can be part of a daily meditation practice. Make meditation one of those things that you deem essential to your life, because it is. Put meditation on your daily to-do list, and you'll still have time for the other things. Truly, there are few things that are more important than meditating. It will put everything else you do in perspective and make doing those things more enjoyable.

I'm going to make another, perhaps more radical, suggestion, which will enhance the quality of your life and help you be more centered throughout your week: Take Sundays off. There's a reason that many have followed this custom. The reason is that unless time is carved out to relax and be, including being with family and loved ones, we aren't likely to take the time, at least not enough time.

With technology continually linking us to others and the world, including our world of work, we periodically need to unplug and recuperate. Unplugging ourselves from our technology and to-do list one day a week is a way to ensure that we connect with our spiritual self.

Making this one change will transform your life for the better and help you stay balanced. It will help you balance the doing with being. When doing isn't balanced with being, we become hostage to the ego's desires and fears, its perception of lack (including a lack of time), and its way of being in the world, which is competitive and self-centered.

If we balance doing with being, our doing will flow more from our being. This is why I said that making time to just be will transform your life: It will take the ego out of the driver's seat and make room for your being to move you instead.

The ego and the heart are likely to make different choices and create different lives and lifestyles. What might your life look like if your heart instead of your ego were driving your actions most of the time? We don't have a lot of models for this because we live in an ego-driven culture, meaning that most people are not in touch with their heart to the extent that they could be. Hence, the rat race.

If you're ready to live a more heart-centered life, then making time daily to meditate and taking one day off a week to discover the wellspring of love, wonder, and delight at your core is the place to start. Doing just these two things will transform your life.

Slowing Down

Slowing down is key to living a more heart-centered life, because shifting gears helps us shift our consciousness and become more present. In fact, it's quite impossible to shift out of the ego without slowing down. We can't be present and live as Presence and still rush around, glued to our cell phone while trying to do six other things at once. When you know Presence, you don't even want to live like that, because you realize that you won't stay present for long if you do.

The biggest stumbling block to slowing down is the perception that you won't have enough time to do everything you need to do. But slowing down can actually leave you with more time, not less. Hurrying is counterproductive because it's stressful. Stress creates emotions, and emotions are exhausting and take time to process or cope with. To deal with stress, we might stop at a bakery for a cupcake, call a friend to complain to, or go on a shopping spree. The ways we cope with stress take up time! Hurrying also makes us more prone to mistakes and accidents, and you know what those do to your plans. Besides, hurrying doesn't feel good. So how is hurrying good?

Of course, we have to hurry sometimes, but making that our usual speed doesn't help us achieve our goals; it only wears us out and makes us scattered and cranky. By slowing down and being more present, we can get just as much done or more and feel better doing it, with energy to spare—and no negative emotions to deal with.

When you slow down and become more present, your life won't fall apart—on the contrary. But it could change. You might make some different choices about how you spend your time and end up with more time to do what you'd really like to do. Or maybe you'll continue doing what you've been doing but with more enjoyment. What you choose to do once you slow down depends on whether what you were doing was motivated by the ego or your heart.

Our culture needs to make a similar shift from the ego's values to the heart's. Our culture keeps us locked into egoic values and the materialistic lifestyle that those values create. The unhealthy lifestyle that many of us are living seems normal, even desirable, perhaps because we don't know what the alternative looks or feels like. Or we may know, but out of fear, we don't feel that we can live differently. But, of course, there are already many who are living more consciously. It's important to seek out models of healthy living and move away from people who aren't models of this and who don't support us in making the changes we'd like to make.

Slowing down means doing whatever you do more slowly and with more presence. It also means being less busy by cutting out things that aren't necessary or meaningful. This will make room for things that are more nourishing to your soul. Only you can decide what needs to be cut. You can tell by how you feel when you're doing something. Do you feel excited and happy or at least content doing it, or do you feel contracted? The heart shows us what's true to do and not do in any moment. We are meant to follow our joy. We are meant to enjoy life.

It may seem scary at first to choose on this basis, but what have your choices been based on before? If you are unhappy or leading a stressful life, you've been listening to the egoic mind. There's another way to live, and it begins by slowing down, being present, and following your heart.

Making Time for Your Heart's Desires

A life guided by our heart is likely to be centered around developing and using our talents, creative expression, growing, learning, serving, loving, becoming wiser, and contributing to life in some way that feels meaningful. How this will look for you depends on your interests, gifts, personality, the opportunities that present themselves, and what you are guided by your heart to do.

As we become more aligned with our heart, our priorities and interests become clearer and often shift. Things that may not have been a priority may become one, like meditating, playing music, creating art, or participating in a service project; while other activities may fall away. Things you were once interested in may no longer be interesting, and things you once wanted to do, may no longer seem desirable. Some activities you thought were necessary may now be seen as unnecessary.

Some activities are soul-nourishing, while others are soul-stripping. The things that nourish us are the things we love to do. They enliven us and connect us with our true nature. Things that are soul-stripping do the opposite: They drain our energy and leave us contracted and stressed-out. It might be helpful to make a list of your activities to see how much time you're spending doing things that don't nourish you versus things that do.

Of course, there are many things we need to do to take care of ourselves and those we love, such as showering, eating, grocery shopping, cooking, chauffeuring our children, and feeding our pets. Although these activities may not be particularly fun, they aren't soul-stripping, unless our attitude makes them so. They are more like medicine. Medicine is not exciting and not always pleasant, but it's good for us. It's good to take care of what needs to be done. When we do, it feels good—

we feel good. Doing what needs to be done is not soul-stripping and, with the right attitude, can be enjoyable.

Whether things that need to be done feel enjoyable or not depends on how present we are when we're doing them. Washing and slicing the strawberries can be an experience of beauty and peace if you are very present to it. Any mundane, routine task that is done with presence can bring forth delight and gratitude.

"I'd rather be fishing" is no attitude to bring to something we're doing. If we have to do something, we might as well make it as enjoyable as possible. We do that by slowing down and giving whatever we're doing our full attention instead of hurrying through it and thinking about something else, like fishing. It is in our power to make any moment pleasant—or not—by choosing where we put our attention.

So much for medicine. What are the things that nourish your soul? You might want to make a list of what you love to do, not just now, but what you've loved doing in the past, because those are often the things we still long to do. This is such an important question. If we aren't aware of what we love to do, we're likely to fill up our time doing things that don't nourish us, like watching TV, shopping, or chatting mindlessly.

Most people's souls are nourished by the same things: being in nature, meditating, spending time with loved ones, listening to music, making music, creating, singing, dancing, or engaging in other physical activities or hobbies for the pure pleasure of it. What would you love to do more of? How would that feel? How do you stop yourself from doing those things? How can you begin to incorporate them into your life?

How much of your time do you spend doing the things you love? What is life without these things? Many people are depressed because they don't make room to do what they love.

They may not even know what that is. Then life becomes a chore, dry, flavorless. It becomes all about responsibilities and work, the endless to-do list. When we don't make room for renewal, recreation, and reconnection with our spirit, the energy drains out of us. We're like the walking dead.

When life becomes flavorless, to continue with the food metaphor, we often turn to artificial highs — desserts — which may be actual desserts or alcohol, drugs, shopping, gambling, compulsive sex, watching too much TV, and other pleasures that we engage in to try to feel soul-full again.

Such indulgences and addictions are the ego's way of coping with the sense of lack and disconnection from our true nature, which the ego itself created. Unfortunately, such activities only leave us feeling more empty and disconnected. They are soul-stripping and take time away from doing the things that nourish us on a deep level. Once we become involved in more soul-nourishing activities, these indulgences and addictions often naturally fall away.

Soul-stripping activities also include anything that we don't need to do or want to do but do out of obligation. Whenever we attend a social function or say yes to a request from someone because we feel we should, we've committed our time and energy to something that doesn't nourish us. If we do that a lot, we won't have time and energy for what we love to do. Here are a few questions for you to contemplate:

❖ *What soul-stripping or perhaps just unnecessary activities do you engage in?*

❖ *Why do you say yes to them?*

❖ *What beliefs or fears keep you from saying no to them?*

❖ *What do you imagine would happen if you said no? That's what keeps you tied to those activities.*

❖ *How might you use that time and energy instead?*

❖ *Can you give this gift of time and energy to yourself? If not, why not?*

One of the most common types of activities that drain us are interactions with individuals who are unkind, judgmental, argumentative, or negative in other ways. We put up with such people for a number of reasons: out of obligation, because we're trying to fix them, or because we grew up in a negative environment and are therefore willing to accept bad behavior because it feels familiar.

Those with healthy self-esteem say no to negativity out of love for themselves. It doesn't serve us to spend time with those who are caught up in discontentment and dramas of their own making. If you want less stress, one of the first places to start is to avoid, as best you can, those who make you feel contracted and stressed-out.

People can be our greatest hindrance or our greatest help in our growth. Seeking out those who support you in being at peace and following your heart is essential in creating a new life and lifestyle. We get to choose who we spend our time with. This even goes for family members, bosses, and co-workers. Making your heart and peace a priority might mean limiting your interactions with certain people and leaving relationships, jobs, or even a particular profession behind.

We expect too much if we think that we can remain happy and at peace with people and in environments in which that is impossible, except maybe for a saint. However, a saint isn't likely to put him- or herself in such situations. People who are in touch with their true nature and for whom that is primary organize their lives to support that, not only because it feels right, but because not doing so is likely to jeopardize their peace and happiness.

I meet people all the time who believe that being spiritual means you should be able to live in any situation and be peaceful and happy, and that just isn't so. Our heart guides us to create a lifestyle that supports our peace and happiness, not one that takes us away from peace and happiness. We have to honor that which is awakening within us that loves peace and happiness by moving away from environments, situations, and people who do not.

We only have so much time and energy. What will you say no to and what will you say yes to? The answer to this isn't difficult if you listen to your heart and say yes to what nourishes you and no to what doesn't. In taking care of ourselves this way, we are ultimately taking care of the Whole. Everyone benefits.

Explorations

1. Over the next few days, pay attention to where your joy lies. What do you do that you really enjoy? Or what would you like to do that you aren't doing? What makes your heart sing? What keeps you from doing that or from following your heart in other ways? What if you did more of what you love?

2. Think of times when you followed your heart and how that felt. Was it worthwhile? Was your heart trustworthy? Following our heart isn't always easy (because life isn't always easy), and sometimes following our heart leads us into lessons. But when we're following our heart, the sense of rightness and the resources we are given carry us through. Now think of a

time when you didn't follow your heart but you followed an idea or a should instead. How was that? We learn from these experiences too, although that learning comes at a cost to our happiness.

Less Is More

The more present we are to life, the more enjoyment we get out of life. The opposite is also true: The less present we are to life, the less enjoyment we get out of life. This is no doubt why so many are unhappy in our bustling, striving culture. How can we be happy when we're so out of contact with reality?

The ego's world is: "I have to do this or I won't be okay. What will people think of me? I have to look good." *I, I, I.* When you're wrapped up in thoughts about yourself, what you have to do, what others think, and how you look, you aren't happy. When your experience of life is your thoughts, you can't be happy, no matter what you do or how good you look. It's a lost cause.

But we still try. We try by doing the things that we think will make us okay, will make us look good, and will make people like us. Those goals and values become our driving force, what shapes our life. But unfortunately, we will never be okay enough, be good looking enough, or please enough people. The game is rigged against us. The ego always wins.

To be happy, we have to stop playing the ego's game. We have to drop out of these thoughts into reality and discover from there what moves us. When we stop listening to our thoughts about ourselves and stop being moved by them, we discover that something else moves us and has always been moving us to some extent. That is our true self.

We are moved by the force that enlivens us. When we are present, we discover that we still move, speak, work, play, and do the things we're used to doing, but we do them more spontaneously, without having an internal debate about them, and without the influence of the personal identity, the *I, I, I* drumbeat of the mind. What freedom this is! And what a joy.

The less we are involved with the mind, the more happy we are. Less is more. But less is more in the usual sense as well. The happier we are, the less we need what the ego claims we need to be happy: material things, entertainment, addictive pleasures, money, status, recognition, power, fame, security, and comfort. The more present we are, the more content we are simply with what is. This sounds boring and undesirable to the ego, which is why it can take so long for us to discover this secret.

Happiness lies in simply being present. When we fall into Presence, we land in a place of contentment. What does contentment feel like? It feels like peace and gratitude. It feels like an expansion in your heart, which we call love. It feels like all is well and that this moment is perfect just as it is. It feels full and complete. You feel complete. This is it! Isn't this what we're all looking for? It's all right here in simply being present.

When we feel this content, do we need to be entertained, do we need to be busy or go places to entertain ourselves? Do we need to overeat or treat ourselves in other ways? When you are content, you might still choose to do these things, but you won't be compelled to do them out of a sense of lack. When you are present, you are entertained by whatever you do. And you're entertained by just being, by simply experiencing your beingness in meditation or otherwise. Life is much simpler because you need much less to be happy.

Since you feel full and complete, you don't need other people in the way that you might have in the past. You don't need others to make you feel good or to feel loved. You join with others because there's a mutual enjoyment and sharing, not out of obligation or because you need something from them or vice versa. More presence means less time spent in codependent and draining relationships and more spent in relationship with your own sweet Self.

More presence also means a lifestyle of less stuff, which means less shopping, less taking care of things, less house to house your things, a smaller car to transport things, less harm to the environment, and less income needed to buy things. Less income needed means more flexibility in job choice, more freedom to do what you love, and more time to lead a balanced life.

What we're talking about here is a radical change in lifestyle that can lead to a radical change in society, a shift from egoic values to the heart's values. This shift is part of our human evolution and society's. It is inevitable, and it is happening now.

Reassessing Your Relationship to the Media

What holds the egoic values in place to a large extent is the media, particularly television but also movies. Television and movies can inspire, uplift, inform, and take us places we've always wanted to go. Or they can do the opposite: scare, sadden, anger, depress, misinform, and take us places we never wanted to go. Just as we need to be mindful of what people we spend our time with, we need to be mindful of the television and movies we watch, or we'll become more entrenched in the egoic state of consciousness rather than freed from it.

We are conditioned by what we watch, whether we're aware of that or not. The unconscious mind is programmed by images, for better or for worse. For instance, even if you don't approve of violence, watching it affects your state of consciousness. Who can come away from such images feeling good, uplifted, and cared for by a benevolent universe? Who can come away feeling trusting of life rather than afraid of it? And fear, as we have seen, puts us in the pocket of the ego. Is this what we want to teach our children? Is this the truth about life?

We know the value of something by how it makes us feel — by its effect. For instance, if someone says something that contracts you, then you know that it came from that person's ego, and it's activating your ego. On the other hand, if it makes you feel more loving and at peace, then it came from love and peace, and it's activating that within you. Similarly, if you feel contracted while watching something, then it was born from egoic consciousness, and it's activating that within you.

So why do we watch things that contract us? Sometimes it's just a matter of not choosing something else. If that's what we're being fed, we eat it without questioning it. That's the situation with much of what is watched: We are indiscriminately watching it. And our children are indiscriminately watching it, as if it doesn't matter. But it does matter! Once we realize that it matters, we need to be more conscious of our choices, especially what we allow our children to watch.

If we pass on the egoic state of consciousness to our children, not much will change in our world. Do we want happy, peace-loving children or frightened, aggressive children? What we feed them in terms of media matters. Will we let the media train our children into consumerism? Will we let it teach them that they aren't okay the way they are, that they need a nose job or breast implants to be loved, because these are the types of messages they are getting from television and the movies.

The media, for the most part, espouses the ego's values because the media serves the corporations, which produce the goods that the ego wants. Corporations feed off of the ego's sense of lack, of never having enough. If people felt they were fine the way they are, they wouldn't feel they needed many of the products that are being pushed at them. If people stopped believing that material possessions were the route to happiness, our consumer-oriented society would have to orient around other values.

We have so much in the United States, and yet so many aren't happy. We're popping pills and overeating like crazy. Is this happiness? Many are coming to see that we can't sustain this way of life and that it isn't working anyway. So we must begin, one person at a time, to shift from the ego's values and the stress and unhappiness they create to deeper values, such as peace and love. Please give peace a chance.

Summary: Changing Your Lifestyle

* What's most important to you? Make peace and less stress a priority,

* Meditate daily or take time each day to be quiet and just be,

* Do what you do more slowly and with more presence,

* Do one thing at a time. Minimize multitasking,

* Take one day off each week to unplug from technology and your to-do list and do the things that support Presence and make your heart sing, such as walk in nature, sing, pray, listen to music, be creative, play with your children or pets, dance, garden, cook, or give to others in some way,

* Remove yourself from negative or stressful situations and people whenever you can,

❖ Eliminate activities that are soul-stripping, unnecessary, or not important,

❖ Be selective about the television and movies you watch,

❖ Consume fewer material goods.

Three Instructions

I will leave you with three instructions for peace and happiness: slow down, be present, and follow your joy. These instructions directly counter our default position as humans to hurry, worry, and do what we think. They inoculate us against suffering and discontentment and lead us Home, to a place we've always known existed but couldn't touch with the mind.

May all beings live in peace!
Om Shanti, Shanti Om

APPENDIX: Meditation

*From Trusting Life: Overcoming the Fear and Beliefs That Block
Peace and Happiness*

Meditation is the most powerful tool for learning to be more present and learning to live more from our natural state, from the Noticer, or Stillness. This is why meditation has been recommended as a spiritual practice for millennia.

Meditation is, very simply, taking time to practice being present. Meditation quiets the mind and helps us dis-identify from the mind chatter, which enables us to experience our true nature: Stillness. Meditation shows us that another level of consciousness and way of being is possible besides our constricted, limiting, and fearful identities. By giving us a taste of Stillness, meditation fuels our will and strengthens our commitment to breaking free from the egoic state of consciousness.

How to Meditate

Meditation is actually very simple, very enjoyable—and it will change your life. You don't need to sit any particular way or breathe any particular way, unless you want to. Sitting up straight is recommended, but you don't have to do that to benefit from meditation. You don't even have to have a special place to meditate, although sitting in the same place at the same time each day is conducive to a practice of meditation. All you need is a quiet place where you can go and not be disturbed for a while.

The more rules and hurdles you create around meditating, the more likely your mind will talk you out of meditating. So make meditation as easy and comfortable as possible to ensure that you actually do it.

This goes for the kind of meditation you do as well: Meditate in the way that you most enjoy and works best for you. This may seem obvious, but sometimes people force themselves to follow certain techniques because a book or someone they know says that's the way to do it. Meditation doesn't have to be complicated or difficult. Find a way to do it that you enjoy so that you'll want to do it every day.

The purpose of meditation is to quiet the mind so that we can experience what else is here besides our thoughts. The mind can be quieted by focusing on any number of things, which accounts for the various types of meditation. Usually, focusing on the breath or a sensory experience, such as a sound, an image, or physical or energetic sensation, is suggested. Both the breath and the senses are doorways into the Now, or Stillness.

When we focus on the breath or an image, a sound, or a physical or an energetic sensation, the mind naturally becomes more quiet because we can't think and fully sense at the same time. For instance, you can't simultaneously listen to what someone is saying and think. Similarly, you can't be fully absorbed in listening (meditating) to a piece of music and think. The same is true of any sense: If you're fully engaged in sensing something, then that precludes thinking. If you are thinking while you're sensing something, you aren't fully sensing it, although you might still be aware of it.

The goal in meditation is to be fully engaged in sensing and not in thinking. So the simplest instruction for meditation is to be fully engaged with whatever sensory object you've chosen to focus on, including the breath, and whenever your mind wanders from that, gently bring it back to sensing.

You can meditate (focus) on music. Or you can meditate on the sounds in your environment and on the silence in between those sounds. Or you can meditate on a beautiful flower, a sunset, the breeze blowing through the trees, the clouds moving across the sky, or any other beautiful sight that has the capacity to capture your attention. Or you can meditate to the physical and energetic sensations in your body as you're sitting or moving. Tai Chi, Qigong, yoga, and other body-oriented spiritual practices have you focus on the body and the sensations related to positions and movements of the body. Focusing on the breath and the sensations involved in breathing is the most basic and common meditation suggested by spiritual traditions. Focusing on anything other than thoughts puts you in a meditative state.

Different people enjoy different types of meditations. I'm very auditory and find it easy and enjoyable to meditate to music, and I'm not very body-oriented, so practices like yoga are less appealing to me. Experiment and find out what you most enjoy focusing on. The simple instruction, once again, is to put your attention on what you're listening to, looking at, or sensing in some other way, and when you catch yourself thinking, bring your attention back to just sensing.

Of course, you can also focus on what's coming into all of your senses all at once. This is a good way to stay anchored in the Now as you go about your day. During your day, make it a habit to pay attention to what you are sensing rather than to what you're thinking. The result of being more in your body and senses during the day is peace, contentment, happiness—and greater effectiveness. Listening to our thoughts often distracts us from what we're doing and makes us less effective, not only less happy.

How Long to Meditate

Meditating for a half hour a day is a good start, although an hour a day will really make a difference in your life. If a half hour is all you can do, then do that, but do it every day at least once a day. Regularity is very important. We practice being identified with the mind every day, so it makes sense that we also need to practice dis-identifying with the mind every day.

The reason for meditating at least a half hour is that when you first start meditating, it will probably take that long to move out of the mind and into a quieter, more peaceful state, which is the reward of meditating. If you meditate for only fifteen minutes, your mind may still be as busy as when you started, and you might not get to the point where meditation feels worthwhile. You may have to stay with meditation at least a half hour a day for a while before it begins to be rewarding, pleasurable, and easy. But it will be worth the commitment.

There are many things we do that aren't easy, but we do them for the long-term benefits. Fortunately, like many other things, meditation gets easier after you've practiced it awhile. The longer you practice meditation and the more time you spend in meditation, the more established you'll become in being present, and the easier it will be to be present even during your day.

What follows are some practices, inquiries, and specific meditations for you to do to help you develop your ability to be present and experience Stillness:

Inquiries About Meditation

1. <u>Take some time to examine any resistance you may have to meditating.</u> How do you (your ego) feel about meditating regularly? How do your thoughts and beliefs about meditating keep you from meditating? And when you are meditating, what thoughts come up to try to take you away from meditating or discourage you from continuing? You don't have to respond to these thoughts. They aren't really your thoughts, but your ego's thoughts. Recognize them as ploys on the part of the ego to get you to pay attention to the mind and not meditate. You are what is aware of the thoughts going through your mind.

2. <u>Do you believe meditation is valuable?</u> If not, how do you convince yourself that it isn't? If you don't believe meditation is valuable, then you probably won't do it. What do you value? We tend to take time for what we value. Given that, what does what you do with your time and energy say about what you value? Does what you spend your time doing reflect what you really want?

   Notice how the mind devalues meditation. Notice how else the mind might undermine your commitment to becoming freer, happier, and more trusting of life. The mind often drives us in directions that aren't worthy of our time and energy with shoulds, guilt, fear, and desire.

Practices Related to Meditation

1. <u>Notice how uninterested the mind is in the present moment.</u> The mind is fascinated with the past and the future, and it likes to evaluate the present, but the mind finds nothing of

interest in the actual experience of the moment. Notice how persistently your mind makes suggestions for thinking about something or doing something other than just being in the moment and responding to whatever is coming out of the moment. The mind has a job to do, and that job is to keep you out of the Now.

How does your mind attempt to keep you out of the moment? Which tactics are the most successful at getting you to turn away from being in the moment? A memory? A fantasy? A desire? A fear? A should? A judgment? A thought about food, sex, time, work, what you have to do, imperfection, cleanliness, being successful, or how you look? How long do you actually stay in the Now before you go unconscious and rejoin the egoic mind?

2. Notice what's coming out of the Now: As you go about your day, notice what's arising in the Now. Is the ego saying no to that, complaining about it? That could be one of the things happening in the moment. What else is happening? What sensations? What sounds? What are you seeing? What intuitions? What inspirations? What urges? What drives? What impressions? What judgments? What feelings? What desires? What fears? What are you experiencing? Tension? Stress? Relaxation? Contraction? Expansion? Awareness? Presence? Silence? Acceptance? Beauty? Love? Joy? Peace?

Any number of these things could be coming out of the Now. Something is always arising, and something is always being taken in by you. What's happening right now? Notice how the egoic mind tries to co-opt the moment and draw you into being absorbed in thinking again. The egoic mind especially likes to think about the past, the future, what it likes and doesn't like, what there is to do, and other people.

When you catch yourself thinking, bring your awareness back to your sensory experience and to everything else that's coming out of the Now.

Just experience everything you're experiencing without labeling or evaluating it. Let the moment be as it is. You'll discover that action also comes out of the Now, spontaneously and easily. You naturally do what you need to do. You don't need your thoughts to impel you.

3. Experiment with using beauty as a doorway into the Now. Beauty brings us into the Now. When you notice something beautiful, how does it make you feel? It opens your Heart, doesn't it? This is the experience of Stillness. You can always find your way back to Stillness by noticing something beautiful. Make noticing beauty and spending some time with beauty part of your daily practice. Here are some ways to do that:

Choose something beautiful to look at. Give it your full attention. If evaluations, labels, or other thoughts come up about what you're looking at or about anything else, gently bring your attention back to just seeing. Receive the visual impression and experience its impact on your being. How does the experience of seeing without thinking feel energetically? That peace and contentment is who you are!

Alternately, move your gaze from object to object, without letting it rest on any one thing. This is an especially good practice for when you are walking in nature. Keep your eyes moving around your environment. If thoughts arise about what you're seeing or about anything else, notice them, and then go back to seeing and experiencing the impact beauty has on you energetically.

Meditations

Here are a few different kinds of meditations to try out on your own to help you discover how you might enjoy meditating:

On sound: Listen to the sounds around you. Receive the sounds without mentally commenting on them. If you catch yourself thinking, bring yourself back to listening. If you find yourself resisting a sound, such as a barking dog, notice that resistance and then bring yourself back to listening.

Alternately, listen to the silence in between the sounds and in between the thoughts. What do you experience energetically? If you catch yourself describing what you're experiencing mentally or thinking about something else, notice that and then return to the experience of silence. Stay with this experience a while without rushing off to do something else or follow a thought. Notice how pleasurable just listening is. That experience is who you are!

On your breath: Notice the experience of breathing. Notice the feel of the breath as it enters your nose and leaves your nose. Without changing how you breathe in any way, notice how the body breathes rhythmically in and out, effortlessly, softly, gently—and there you are in the Now. If you find yourself thinking about your breathing, your body, or anything else, bring your attention back to the sensory experience of breathing. The more you practice this, the easier it becomes to move into the Now, and the more you'll want to.

On all your senses: What's coming in through your senses right now? What are you experiencing? A sound? A sight? Something touching you? Warmth? Coolness? Air moving? Tension? Pain?

Pleasure? Many sensations are likely to be happening at once. Notice them without labeling them, evaluating them, or thinking about them. If you find your mind doing that, bring your attention back to the experience your senses are bringing you. Experience whatever you're experiencing without judging it or trying to hold on to it or push it away. Let it be the way it is. Experience what it's like to be a receptor. How does that feel energetically?

A Guided Meditation for Being Present

Here is a guided meditation that you can record for yourself to listen to daily or at least a few times a week to help you be more present:

Get very comfortable and relax into whatever position you are in, with your eyes open or closed. This is your special time, so set aside all thoughts, worries, concerns, and to-do lists and just be. Just be here right now without any of that. You don't need these thoughts, and you have never needed them to be who you are and to do what you came here to do. That which you truly are is right here, right now taking care of everything that needs taking care of. Right now, it's time to just be and to discover what just being is like. By just being still and letting go of any thoughts and concerns, you can discover what your true nature is like and what it's like to live as that. You may think you need your thoughts to be and to survive, but they only interfere with being and with becoming what you can be.

Sink down deeper into whatever position you are in and just notice whatever you are aware of. As you listen to these words, notice the effect they have on you... Notice how your body feels... how your being feels... how this experience feels...

As you continue to allow yourself to experience what you are experiencing, notice whatever else you are experiencing...

Now, with your eyes open, notice the beauty that exists in this moment. How is beauty showing itself to you in this moment? Take a moment to take in whatever beauty you are noticing...

Once again, just notice the experience of you being here now in this moment... Notice how the body feels... Notice how your being feels... Notice how this unique moment in time feels... If a thought comes in, then notice that and then go back to noticing what else is present here in this moment. There's actually a great deal to be aware of, a great deal of richness, beauty, uniqueness, a great deal to be grateful for... If gratitude is coming up, then notice that and continue to notice everything else that's part of this moment. Take some time to just experience, as if you had never seen or heard or been alive before in this world...

Continue to allow your attention to move around, just noticing all that you can notice, just touching that experience and then noticing what else is here. Your mind might want to tell a story or comment about or judge what you're noticing because that's what minds do. When that's happening, just notice that. Thoughts are part of experience, but they are just a small part of experience – and not very true. They're stories we tell ourselves about experience, but they lack the richness and aliveness of the real experience, of really experiencing life. Continue now to just notice and experience whatever you are noticing and experiencing for as long as you like.

ABOUT the AUTHOR

Gina Lake is the author of over twenty books about awakening to one's true nature, including *From Stress to Stillness, All Grace, In the World but Not of It, The Jesus Trilogy, A Heroic Life, Trusting Life, Embracing the Now, Radical Happiness,* and *Choosing Love.* She is also a gifted intuitive with a master's degree in counseling psychology and over twenty-five years' experience supporting people in their spiritual growth. Her website offers information about her books and online course, a free ebook, a blog, and audio and video recordings:

RadicalHappiness.com

Awakening Now Online Course

It's time to start living what you've been reading about. Are you interested in delving more deeply into the teachings in Gina Lake's books, receiving ongoing support for waking up, and experiencing the power of Christ Consciousness transmissions? You'll find that and much more in the Awakening Now online course:

This course was created for your awakening. The methods presented are powerful companions on the path to enlightenment and true happiness. Awakening Now will help you experience life through fresh eyes and discover the delight of truly being alive. This 100-day inner workout is packed with both time-honored and original practices that will pull the rug out from under your ego and wake you up. You'll immerse yourself in materials, practices, guided meditations, and inquiries that will transform your consciousness. And in video webinars, you'll receive transmissions of Christ Consciousness, which are a direct current of love and healing that will accelerate your evolution and help you break through to a new level of being. By the end of 100 days, you will have developed new habits and ways of being that will result in being more richly alive and present and greater joy and equanimity.

www.RadicalHappiness.com/online-courses

More Books by Gina Lake

Available in paperback, ebook, and audiobook formats.

In the World but Not of It: New Teachings from Jesus on Embodying the Divine: From the Introduction, by Jesus: "What I have come to teach now is that you can embody love, as I did. You can become Christ within this human life and learn to embody all that is good within you. I came to show you the beauty of your own soul and what is possible as a human. I came to show you that it is possible to be both human and divine, to be love incarnate. You are equally both. You walk with one foot in the world of form and another in the Formless. This mysterious duality within your being is what this book is about." This book is another in a series of books dictated to Gina Lake by Jesus.

Embracing the Now: Finding Peace and Happiness in What Is. The Now—this moment—is the true source of happiness and peace and the key to living a fulfilled and meaningful life. *Embracing the Now* is a collection of essays that can serve as daily reminders of the deepest truths. Full of clear insight and wisdom, *Embracing the Now* explains how the mind keeps us from being in the moment, how to move into the Now and stay there, and what living from the Now is like. It also explains how to overcome stumbling blocks to being in the Now, such as fears, doubts, misunderstandings, judgments, distrust of life, desires, and other conditioned ideas that are behind human suffering.

All Grace: New Teachings from Jesus on the Truth About Life. Grace is the mysterious and unseen movement of God upon creation, which is motivated by love and indistinct from love. *All Grace* was given to Gina Lake by Jesus and represents his wisdom and understanding of life. It is about the magnificent and incomprehensible force behind life, which created life, sustains it, and operates within it as you and me and all of creation. *All Grace* is full of profound and life-changing truth.

The Jesus Trilogy. In this trilogy by Jesus, are three jewels, each shining in its own way and illuminating the same truth: You are not only human but divine, and you are meant to flourish and love one another. In words that are for today, Jesus speaks intimately and directly to the reader of the secrets to peace, love, and happiness. He explains the deepest of all mysteries: who you are and how you can live as he taught long ago. The three books in *The Jesus Trilogy* were dictated to Gina Lake by Jesus and include *Choice and Will, Love and Surrender,* and *Beliefs, Emotions, and the Creation of Reality.*

Living in the Now: How to Live as the Spiritual Being That You Are. The 99 essays in *Living in the Now* will help you realize your true nature and live as that. They answer many questions raised by the spiritual search and offer wisdom on subjects such as fear, anger, happiness, aging, boredom, desire, patience, forgiveness, acceptance, love, commitment, meditation, being present, emotions, trusting your Heart, and many other deep subjects. These essays will help you become more conscious, present, happy, loving, grateful, at peace, and fulfilled.

Radical Happiness: A Guide to Awakening provides the keys to experiencing the happiness that is ever-present and not dependent on circumstances. This happiness comes from realizing that who you think you are is not who you really are. *Radical Happiness* describes the nature of the egoic state of consciousness and how it interferes with happiness, what awakening and enlightenment are, and how to live in the world after awakening.

Return to Essence: How to Be in the Flow and Fulfill Your Life's Purpose describes how to get into the flow and stay there and how to live life from there. Being in the flow and not being in the flow are two very different states. One is dominated by the ego-driven mind, which is the cause of suffering, while the other is the domain of Essence, the Divine within each of us. You are meant to live in the flow. The flow is the experience of Essence—your true self—as it lives life through you and fulfills its purpose for this life.

Getting Free: Moving Beyond Negativity and Limiting Beliefs. To a large extent, healing our conditioning involves changing our relationship to our mind and discovering who we really are. *Getting Free* will help you do that. It will also help you reprogram your mind; clear negative thoughts and self-images; use meditation, prayer, forgiveness, and gratitude; work with spiritual forces to assist healing and clear negativity; and heal entrenched issues from the past.

A Heroic Life: New Teachings from Jesus on the Human Journey. *A Heroic Life* shows you how to overcome the ego's false beliefs and face the ego's fears. It provides you with both a perspective and a map to help you successfully and happily navigate life's challenges and live heroically. This book is another in a series of books dictated to Gina Lake by Jesus.

Choosing Love: Moving from Ego to Essence in Relationships. Having a truly meaningful relationship requires choosing love over your conditioning, that is, your ideas, fantasies, desires, images, and beliefs. *Choosing Love* describes how to move beyond conditioning, judgment, anger, romantic illusions, and differences to the experience of love and oneness with another. It explains how to drop into the core of your Being, where Oneness and love exist, and be with others from there.

Trusting Life: Overcoming the Fear and Beliefs That Block Peace and Happiness. Fear and distrust keep us from living the life we were meant to live, and they are the greatest hurdles to seeing the truth about life—that it is good, abundant, supportive, and potentially joyous. *Trusting Life* is a deep exploration into the mystery of who we are, why we suffer, why we don't trust life, and how to become more trusting. It offers tools for overcoming the fear and beliefs that keep us from falling in love with life.

For more information, please visit the "Books" page at

www.RadicalHappiness.com

Made in the USA
San Bernardino, CA
04 October 2018